WHAT'S OUT THERE

WHAT'S OUT THERE

IMAGES FROM HERE TO THE EDGE OF THE UNIVERSE

BY
MARY K. BAUMANN
WILL HOPKINS
LORALEE NOLLETTI
MICHAEL SOLURI

FOREWORD BY
STEPHEN HAWKING

ASTRONOMY CONSULTANT
RAY VILLARD

DUNCAN BAIRD PUBLISHERS

LONDON

WHAT'S OUT THERE

First published in the United Kingdom
and Ireland in 2005 by
Duncan Baird Publishers Ltd
Sixth Floor
Castle House
75–76 Wells Street
London W1T 3QH

This book is dedicated to Mark Levine and
to Andre, Patrick and Gabriel Soluri

Credits at Duncan Baird Publishers
Managing Editor: Christopher Westhorp
Managing Designer: Justin Ford

Produced by Hopkins/Baumann
Designers: Will Hopkins and
  Mary K. Baumann
Picture Editor and Astronomer Liaison:
  Michael Soluri
Editor: Paula Glatzer
Managing Editor: Jennifer Dixon
Science Consultant: Ellis D. Miner, Ph.D.
Additional Text: Ira Mothner and Martha Fay
Colour Management Consultant:
  Son Do, Rods and Cones
Icons: John Baxter

British Library Cataloguing-in-Publication Data:
A CIP record for this book is available from
the British Library

10 9 8 7 6 5 4 3 2 1

ISBN-10: 1-84483-250-3
ISBN-13: 9-781844-832507

Inquires regarding WHAT'S OUT THERE contact:
<hopkinsbaumann.com> or <solurispace.com>

Colour reproduction by Colourscan, Singapore
Printed in China by Imago

Note: Any reference herein to the unit
of a billion indicates a thousand million
rather than a million million.

**ROSETTE NEBULA (NGC 2237)
IN THE CONSTELLATION
MONOCEROS**

GLOWING FROM THE ULTRAVIOLET
LIGHT OF YOUNG, HOT BLUE
STARS, THE NEBULA IS A
PROMINENT STAR-FORMING
REGION. STRONG STELLAR WINDS
ARE CLEARING THE CENTER.

VISIBLE-LIGHT IMAGE
THROUGH 3 FILTERS
(REPRESENTATIVE COLOR)

NSF 0.9M TELESCOPE
AT KITT PEAK NATIONAL
OBSERVATORY, NOAO

3 MARCH 1999

1,500 LIGHT-YEARS
FROM EARTH

THE NEVER-ENDING QUEST

AT THE RISK OF INCURRING THE fate of Prometheus, who stole fire from the ancient gods for human use, I believe we can, and should, try to explore and understand the universe. Our knowledge of the universe is constantly expanding, due in large part to our ever-improving technology.

In the last hundred years, we have made spectacular advances in our understanding, and probed deeper and deeper into space in order to further our knowledge. We have put men on the Moon, landed robots on Mars and sent probes out to the farthest reaches of our solar system. Voyager 1, for example, has been traveling for more than 27 years, and is now sending images back to us from approximately eight billion miles (13 billion km) away. This quest for information is key to our advancement, and the data these probes and satellites send us is not only informative, but deeply inspiring.

The images in this book represent some of the most up-to-date and high-definition data available. It is worth considering, that as spectacular as they are, they represent only the minute segment of the universe that man has been able to investigate. It is currently estimated that there may be up to 150 billion galaxies in the universe; the majority of these images are taken from just one – ours.

I do not believe we will ever reach the end of our quest for a complete understanding of the universe, and in a way, I'm glad. Science after finding all the answers would be like mountaineering after Everest. The human race needs an intellectual challenge. It would be boring to have nothing left to discover.

STEPHEN HAWKING
CAMBRIDGE, ENGLAND
FALL 2004

STEPHAN'S QUINTET
GALAXIES PULLED TOGETHER
BY GRAVITATIONAL FORCE
VISIBLE-LIGHT IMAGE
GEMINI OBSERVATORY
8M MIRROR
12 AUGUST 2004
300 MILLION LIGHT-YEARS
FROM EARTH

START HERE

THIS IS THE VIEW FROM EARTH OF OUR HOME GALAXY, THE MILKY WAY

THE MILKY WAY GALAXY IS OUR celestial hometown. Think of it as a vast metropolis, with as many as 200 billion stars. But it is just one of a possible 150 billion galaxies in the universe. And it is where our solar family — Earth, the Sun and our eight sister planets — are found.

We're relative newcomers. Our solar system was formed no

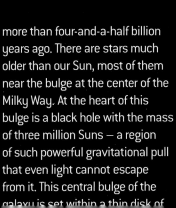

A PANORAMIC
EDGE-ON VIEW OF
THE MILKY WAY
FROM EARTH
INFRARED COMPOSITE IMAGE
2MASS
APRIL 1997–MARCH 2001
25,000 LIGHT-YEARS
TO THE GALACTIC CENTER

more than four-and-a-half billion years ago. There are stars much older than our Sun, most of them near the bulge at the center of the Milky Way. At the heart of this bulge is a black hole with the mass of three million Suns – a region of such powerful gravitational pull that even light cannot escape from it. This central bulge of the galaxy is set within a thin disk of

stars about 100,000 light-years wide (a light-year is 5.9 trillion miles/ 9.5 trillion km).

We and our Sun are located far from the center of the metropolis. We're in a kind of suburb, out on a long arm of the spiral-shaped Milky Way Galaxy. The view is great. From our place in space, we can look both "in," toward the galaxy's center, and

"out" – as far into space and time as modern telemetry can take us. Still, the vast number of stars we see with the naked eye are all neighbors, fellow residents of the Milky Way.

Galaxies (after the Greek word "gala" for milk) come in many different sizes and several shapes. And all are made, not only of stars, but also of gas

and dust and the invisible material astronomers call "dark matter." We can't see dark matter, but as much as 90 percent of a galaxy's mass consists of it.

The Milky Way is not alone in our sector of the universe. It belongs to a small cluster of galaxies called the Local Group, which has some three dozen known members.

ASTEROID

Asteroids are space rubble, dark rocky fragments created during the formation of the solar system almost five billion years ago. This orbiting debris is the leftover material that didn't quite come together to make a planet or a moon.

Asteroids come in irregular shapes and sizes. Some are larger than the length of Italy, while others are less than a few city blocks in diameter.

Most asteroids orbit the Sun in the gap between Mars and Jupiter, which is known as the Asteroid Belt. Asteroid orbits are usually stable for millions of years. However, because asteroids are so small and there are so many of them, their orbits are not confined to a single, ecliptic plane like those of planets. Asteroid orbits span a large range of inclinations due to the long-term effects of the gravitational pull of Jupiter, Mars, or nearby asteroids.

Tumbling through space, have asteroids ever hit Earth? It is believed that a huge asteroid or comet slammed into what is now the Yucatan peninsula 65 million years ago. Asteroid hits are rare, but meteoroid hits occur almost continually, adding tons of material to our planet every day. Meteoroids are often the offspring of asteroids or comets.

A

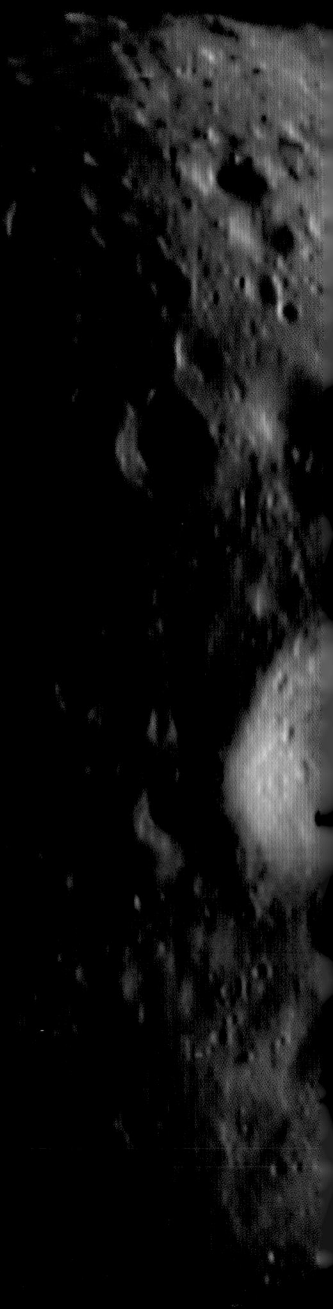

ASTEROID EROS

21 MILES (33KM) LONG,
8 MILES (13KM) WIDE
AND 8 MILES THICK

A MOSAIC OF VISIBLE-LIGHT
AND INFRARED IMAGES
DRAPED OVER A
COMPUTER MODEL
OF THE ASTEROID SHAPE

NEAR SHOEMAKER PROBE

124 MILES (200KM)
FROM NEAR SHOEMAKER

29 FEBRUARY 2000

160 MILLION MILES
(258 MILLION KM)
FROM EARTH

A

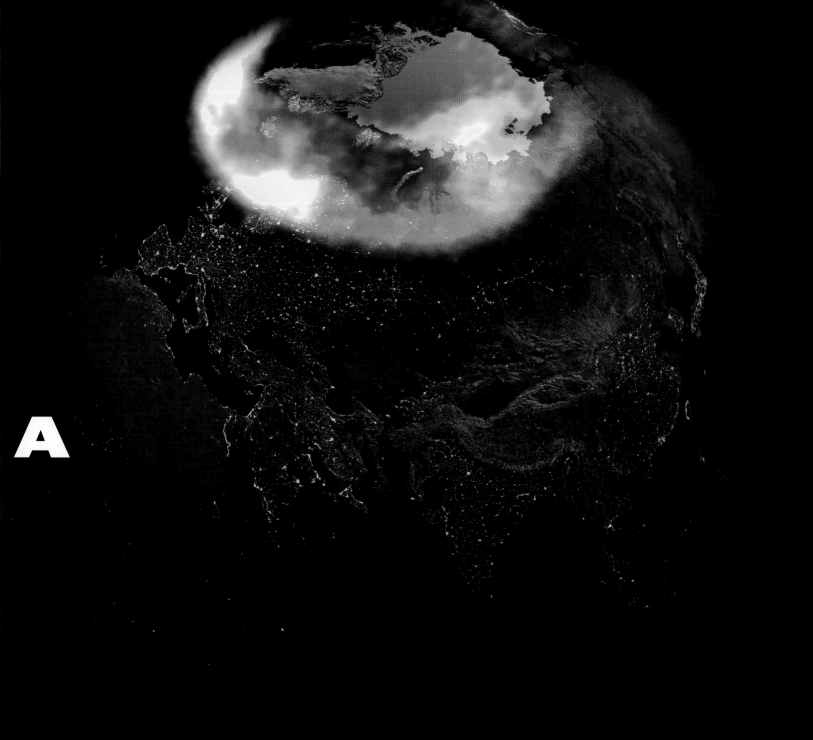

A

AURORA

AURORA BOREALIS

ULTRAVIOLET IMAGE
OF THE AURORA OVERLAID
ON A VISIBLE-LIGHT
IMAGE OF EARTH

AURORA: NASA POLAR
SPACECRAFT
EARTH: TERRA AND
DMSP SATELLITES

17 SEPTEMBER 2000

AURORA: 34,000 MILES
(54,000KM) FROM
POLAR SPACECRAFT

EARTH: 150 MILES (241KM)
BELOW AURORA

Auroras are the biggest and most spectacular light shows in Earth's atmosphere – beautiful but potentially dangerous spectacles. Like fireworks over Shanghai on the Chinese New Year or Rio de Janeiro during Carnival, brilliant and changing colors paint parts of the sky.

Named for the Roman goddess of dawn, auroras usually appear in the skies above the Earth's North and South poles –

named respectively the aurora borealis or northern lights and the aurora australis or southern lights. While they seem to be mirror images of each other, there are significant differences in timing, intensity and location.

Auroras occur when electrons and protons from coronal mass ejections are propelled through space and crash into atoms in a planet's upper atmosphere. Something electric happens

A

there. As the solar particles collide with the planet's oxygen and nitrogen atoms, the particles give up some of their energy to the atoms. As they return to normal, the atoms give off energy in the form of colorful glowing light. The energy from the solar particles also wreaks havoc with satellites and terrestrial power grids.

An aurora's colors depend on what atoms are struck by electrons at what height. Green lights result from oxygen emissions at 60 miles (100km). At higher altitudes oxygen emissions produce red lights. Neutral (un-ionized) nitrogen produces pink lights, while ionized nitrogen creates the rare blue or violet lights.

The lights typically adorn the cold skies above our polar regions. Auroras follow Earth's magnetic field lines, which direct the energetic electrons to the auroral oval, the area that encircles each pole. Auroras have also been observed on other planets, including Saturn and Jupiter. Auroras occur on these planets because they have powerful magnetic fields and atmospheres that can be electrified by charged particles.

**AURORA BOREALIS AND
AURORA AUSTRALIS
ON SATURN**

AURORAL CURTAINS
AT POLES RISE 1,000 MILES
(1,600KM) ABOVE CLOUDS

ULTRAVIOLET IMAGE

HUBBLE SPACE
TELESCOPE
(EARTH-ORBITING)

OCTOBER 1997

810 MILLION MILES
(1.3 BILLION KM)
FROM EARTH

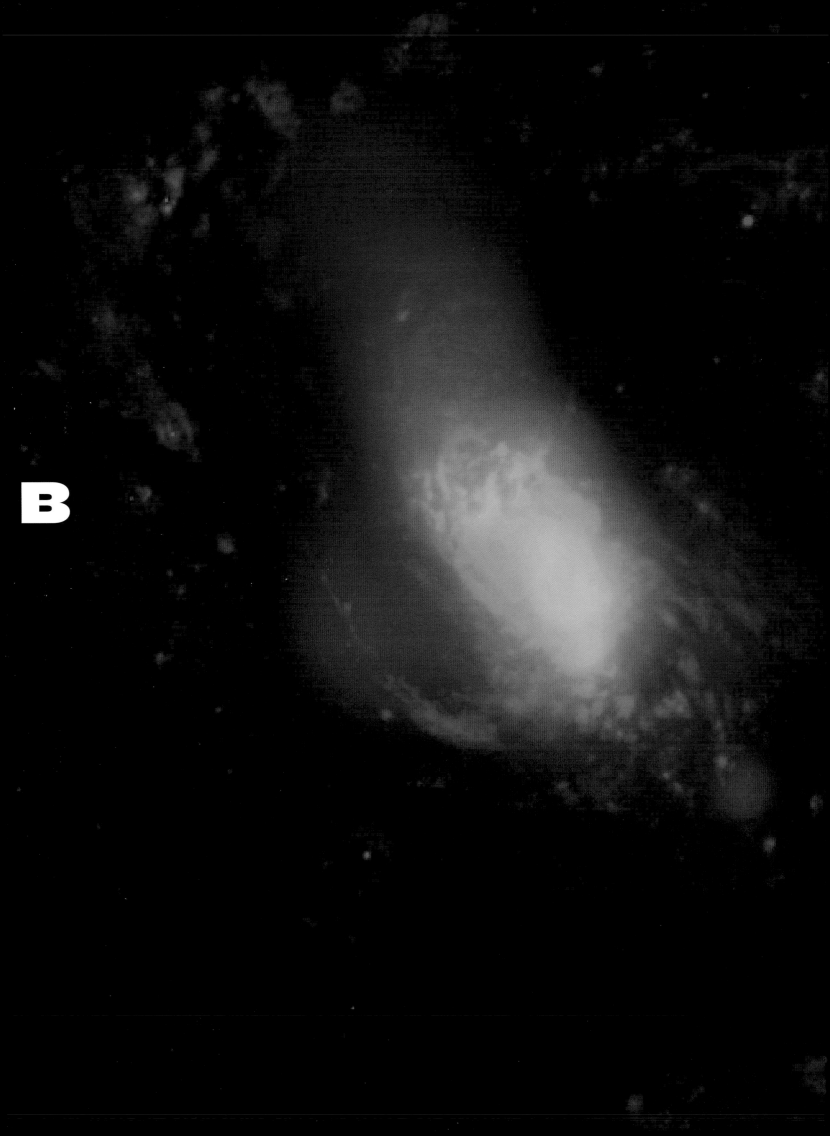

BLACK HOLE

BLACK HOLES ARE COLLAPSED pieces of our universe where time and space as we know it cease to exist. All that identifies a black hole is a remnant gravitational field that is so intense that nothing can escape once it is sucked in, even light. Today black holes are more than a theoretical curiosity. Astronomers have discovered them hidden in the cores of galaxies, and much closer to home in our galactic suburbs.

Most black holes form when a massive star runs out of fuel and explodes in a supernova. If the surviving stellar core is three times more massive than our Sun, nothing can stop it from imploding. The result is a singularity, a scrunched piece of the universe with almost no volume and infinite density. Surrounding the singularity is a boundary called the event horizon. The more massive the black hole the bigger the event horizon. But the singularity always remains smaller than the period at the end of this sentence. Anything that crosses the event horizon is trapped forever because the needed escape velocity is faster than the velocity of light — the universe's speed limit.

The term "black hole" was coined in 1967 by astronomer John Wheeler. But black holes were theorized a century before Einstein's theory of general relativity predicted the warping of space and distortion of light by gravity. In the mid-1990s, the Hubble Space Telescope confirmed the existence of black holes in the centers of galaxies by measuring the whirlpool motion of stars, dust and gas around them.

Telescopes cannot actually see material falling near an event horizon. To an outside observer, time would appear to stop — whatever is falling into the black hole would look frozen in space.

This is because an intense gravitational field slows the flow of time. Hubble has viewed the onset of this effect, called a "light decay train."

An even more paradoxical idea, called "Hawking radiation" after theoretical physicist Stephen Hawking, states that black holes eventually vanish because they leak away mass in the form of particles. Empty space is constantly churning with "virtual particles" — pairs of particles with opposite charges that abruptly annihilate each other and vanish. If it happens at a black hole's event horizon, one particle might fall in before being annihilated. To conserve mass in the universe, the particle that escapes would have to be subtracted from the mass of the black hole. According to this theory, every black hole must constantly radiate energy and will eventually disappear.

In 2004 Hawking took this idea a step further by saying that information about whatever falls into a black hole — a book, a car or a breadbox — somehow survives. This means that energy flowing from a black hole actually carries information about what fell in, although in mangled form. This idea would solve a paradox from quantum theory — that information can never be destroyed in our universe.

GAS BLOWS FROM A HIDDEN BLACK HOLE AT THE CENTER OF GALAXY NGC 1068

COMPOSITE X-RAY AND VISIBLE-LIGHT IMAGE

CHANDRA X-RAY OBSERVATORY (EARTH-ORBITING)

4 DECEMBER 2000

50 MILLION LIGHT-YEARS FROM EARTH

BLUE SUPERGIANT

THE MOST MASSIVE AND BRILLIANT stars in the sky are blue supergiants. They are about ten times the mass of our Sun, and a few may be more than a hundred times. But these colossal stars are rare. Most stars in our galaxy are smaller than our Sun. Blue supergiants are literally one in a thousand.

Big and bright, blue supergiants stand out in the night sky. The star Rigel, for instance, in the constellation Orion has twenty times the Sun's mass and 60,000 times its brilliance. A supergiant's blue-white color and extraordinary luminance derive from its extreme surface temperature — above 55,000°F (31,000°C), compared to the Sun's surface temperature of 10,300°F (5,700°C).

But a supergiant's brilliance is short-lived by stellar standards. Burning up its gases at a furious rate, it is likely to live 10 million years, while our Sun has a 10-billion-year life span. And when a blue supergiant exhausts its nuclear fuel, it comes to a spectacular end — in a supernova. The core contracts and collapses and the outer layers crash onto it, releasing so much energy that the star is blasted apart. The collapsed core then goes on to either form a black hole or become a neutron star.

B

**BLUE SUPERGIANT SHER 25
IN NEBULA NGC 3603**
(UPPER LEFT OF CENTRAL CLUSTER IN RING)

THE BLUE RING AND BIPOLAR OUTFLOW (OR BLOBS) ARE GASEOUS LEFTOVERS FROM STAR BIRTH

VISIBLE-LIGHT IMAGE

HUBBLE SPACE TELESCOPE (EARTH-ORBITING)

5 MARCH 1999

20,000 LIGHT-YEARS FROM EARTH

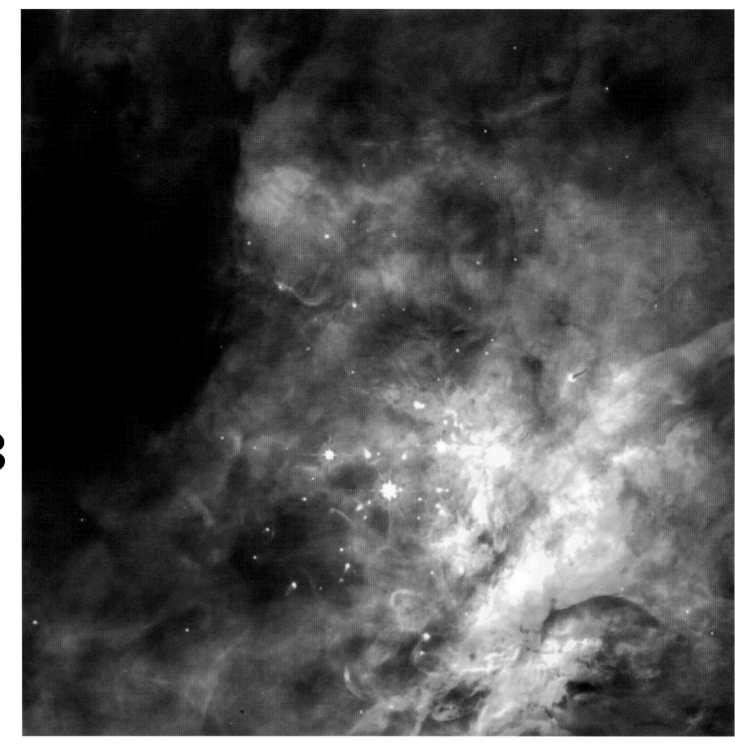

B

BROWN DWARF

BROWN DWARFS SURROUND THE MASSIVE CENTRAL STARS OF THE TRAPEZIUM CLUSTER IN THE GREAT NEBULA OF ORION

BROWN DWARFS, TOO DIM TO BE SEEN IN VISIBLE LIGHT (LEFT), POP OUT IN INFRARED (RIGHT)

LEFT: VISIBLE-LIGHT MOSAIC (COLOR ADDED)
RIGHT: NEAR-INFRARED IMAGE

HUBBLE SPACE TELESCOPE (EARTH-ORBITING)

LEFT: 1994–1995
RIGHT: 17 JANUARY 1998

1,500 LIGHT-YEARS FROM EARTH

BROWN DWARFS ARE WHAT astronomers call "failed stars." They have about the same diameter as Jupiter but at least ten times the mass. However, their mass is still too low to produce the high temperatures necessary for nuclear fusion. Cool and dim, with a surface temperature below 4,500 °F (2,500 °C), brown dwarfs are a hundred thousand to a million times fainter than our Sun, at least for most of their lives. For a brief period while young, they are relatively bright yet they are still a hundred to a thousand times less luminous than our central star.

The faint light may explain why no brown dwarfs were discovered before 1995. Since then, telescopes with sensitive infrared detectors have located several hundred. In a celestial population that includes both stars and brown dwarfs, if there are a hundred billion stars in our galaxy there are about five to ten billion brown dwarfs.

B

The same process that forms normal stars also forms brown dwarfs. But in their case, there is just not enough gas available to reach true stellar mass and they are unable to fuse hydrogen. Early in life, however, brown dwarfs are capable of generating energy by burning deuterium (heavy hydrogen). But when this gas is exhausted after several tens of millions of years, the release of gravitational energy allows brown dwarfs to continue to glow as they slowly contract.

In 2004, a planet-forming disk was spotted by the Spitzer Space Telescope around a brown dwarf only 15 times the mass of Jupiter. The brown dwarf, known as OTS 44, is an extremely low-mass version near the dividing line between planets and stars. "It's fascinating to think that there could be miniature solar systems out there in which planets orbit objects that themselves are almost as small as planets," said Dr Kevin Luhman of the Harvard-Smithsonian Center for Astrophysics and lead investigator of the study.

Planet-forming disks provide the construction materials for planets to coalesce. The dusty disk surrounding OTS 44 has enough mass to build a small gas giant planet and a few rocky ones. Could life happen in such a system? If a life-friendly planet could form, it would need to accommodate diminishing temperatures. A planet like ours, in order to maintain a supply of liquid water, would have to be closer to the brown dwarf than Earth is to our Sun.

The search for invisible bodies such as brown dwarfs reflects a trend in astronomy toward examining smaller, dimmer sections of the sky. It is there, tucked into the less flashy corners of the cosmos, where life is most likely to be.

CHROMOSPHERE

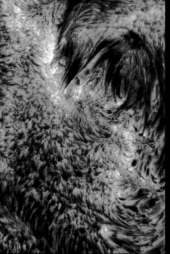

SPICULES
H-ALPHA,
VISIBLE-LIGHT IMAGE
(COLOR ADDED)
SWEDISH 1M
SOLAR TELESCOPE
16 JUNE 2003
93 MILLION MILES
(150 MILLION KM)
FROM EARTH

DERIVED FROM THE GREEK, chromosphere means sphere of color. This layer of the Sun's atmosphere gets its name from the faint red light it gives off, like the flickering edge of a bonfire. Normally invisible because of the glare from the Sun's surface, the chromosphere can be seen as a bright red crescent during a total eclipse.

Even though the chromosphere is 1,500 miles (2,400km) thick, it is thin by Sun standards, like patterns of ink on a printed page. The chromosphere is the outer layer of the Sun's surface, located above the photosphere and below the corona. The photosphere is the visible layer of the Sun – the part where the light that we see is emitted. Above the relatively cool photosphere, the chromosphere rises in temperature to 17,500°F (9,700°C).

The chromosphere is irregular. Narrow bursts of gas jets called spicules (above) shoot 3,000 miles (4,800km) above the surface at speeds up to 30,000mph (50,000kph).

C

CHROMOSPHERE
ULTRAVIOLET IMAGE
(COLOR ADDED)
SUMER TELESCOPE
ON SOHO SPACECRAFT
92 MILLION MILES
(148 MILLION KM)
FROM SOHO
12 MAY 1996

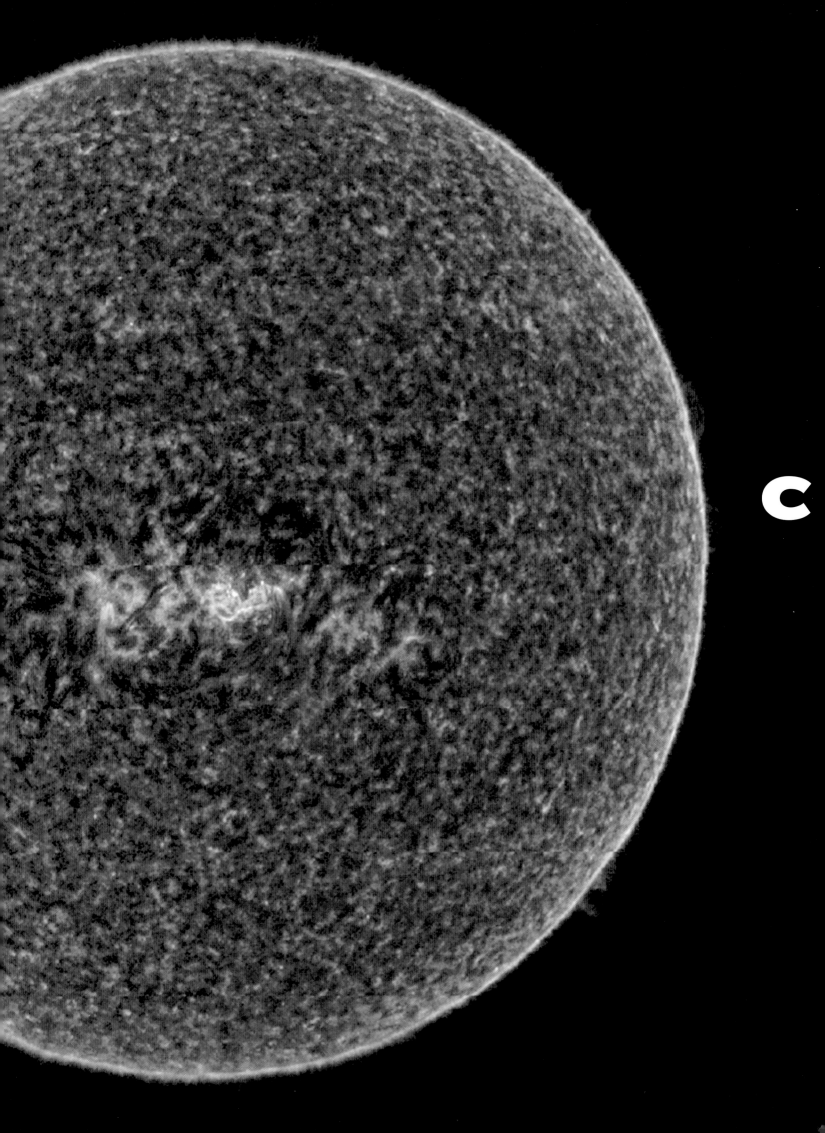

c

CLUSTER

CELESTIAL BODIES ARE A companionable lot. They hang out together, and they tend to hang out with their own kind. Stars, for example, come in clusters, and there are two types. Young stars are most likely to be found in the smaller, more loosely structured "open" clusters, while older stars generally make up the more highly structured "globular" clusters.

The young stars in an open cluster were all formed at approximately the same time within the same cloud of dust and gas. Because of their youth, these stars burn hot and bright. The clusters they form are loose and uncrowded. This is because of the weakness of their gravitational fields, which are often too frail to keep them together.

Open clusters tend to be found along the arms of spiral galaxies, where there is new star formation. There are many open clusters in our own Milky Way. Among them are the stars of the Pleiades (below) in the constellation Taurus – the easiest cluster to spot with the naked eye.

Globular clusters, by contrast, are huge. They contain a tightly knit throng of stars – from 100,000 to one million – and are usually spherical in shape. Among the oldest structures in the universe, globular clusters were the first inhabitants of our galaxy. They are generally found outside the galaxy's disk, far from the star-forming regions. They are not involved in the galaxy's general rotation. Instead, they follow orbits of their own around the galactic center. In the Milky Way, about 150 globular clusters travel above and below the galactic plane in the halo, the spherical area that envelops the galaxy.

Globular clusters hold some of the oldest stars in our galaxy. The biggest and brightest of these clusters is Omega Centauri (right), with stars 12 billion years old. Some 17,000 light-years away, it resembles a small cloud in the southern sky. It, too, can be seen with the naked eye.

Omega Centauri contains several million stars, so densely packed that they occasionally collide. When they do collide, it is believed that they merge to create hot blue stars.

THE PLEIADES OPEN STAR CLUSTER IN THE CONSTELLATION TAURUS (LOWER LEFT)
VISIBLE-LIGHT COMPOSITE THROUGH RED, GREEN AND BLUE FILTERS
PALOMAR 48-INCH SCHMIDT TELESCOPE
5 NOVEMBER 1986– 11 SEPTEMBER 1996
440 LIGHT-YEARS FROM EARTH

THE CORE OF GLOBULAR CLUSTER OMEGA CENTAURI (RIGHT)
LOCATED IN THE CONSTELLATION CENTAURUS, THE CLUSTER OF STARS ORBITS AROUND A COMMON CENTER OF GRAVITY
VISIBLE-LIGHT IMAGE
HUBBLE SPACE TELESCOPE (EARTH-ORBITING)
11 JUNE 1997
17,000 LIGHT-YEARS FROM EARTH

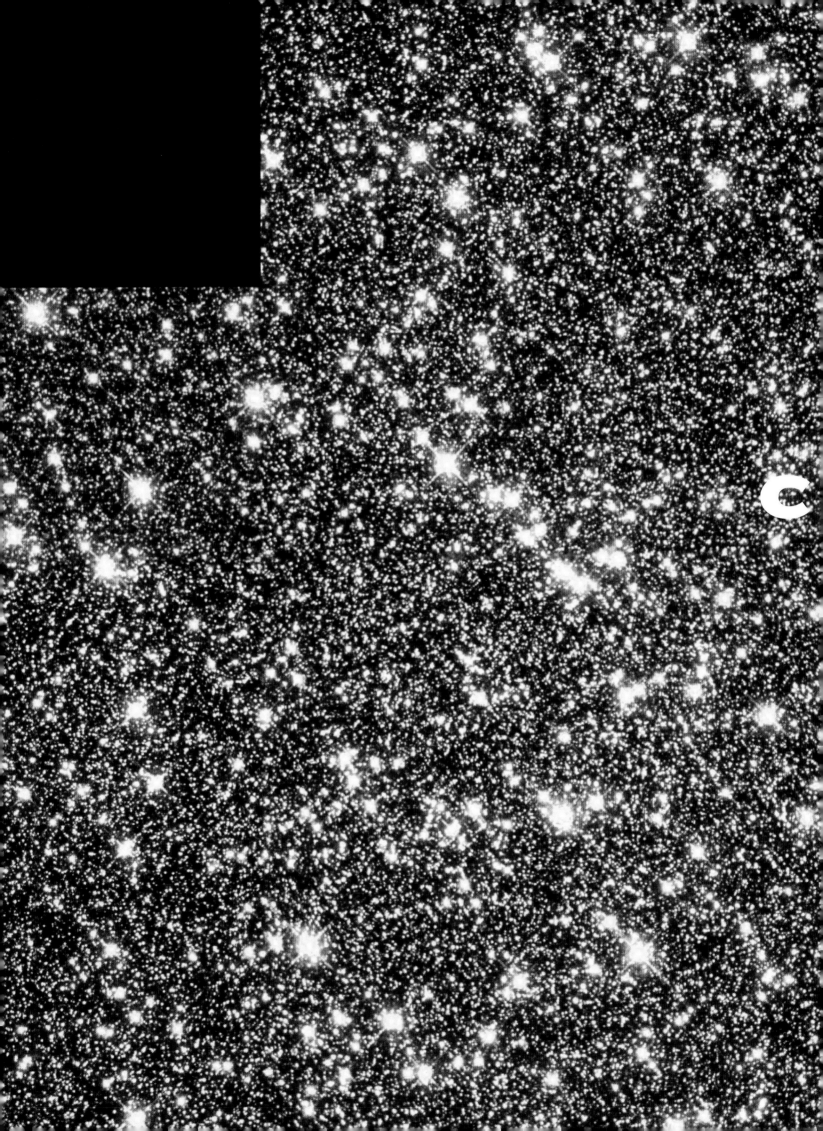

COMET

Comets are like miniplanets, with orbits of their own within our solar system. Irregular balls of ice, dust, rocks and gas just a few miles wide, comets move in long elliptical orbits that bring them close to the Sun either repeatedly (as with Halley's 76-year orbit) or rarely.

A comet's most prominent feature is its dust tail, although comets sometimes form a secondary tail, called an ion tail. The tails generally begin to form when the comet approaches within a few hundred miles of the Sun. The Sun heats a comet's nucleus, causing ice to vaporize and turn to gas that is explosively expelled along with a lot of dust. The dust forms a huge coma or head around the nucleus, often reaching thousands of miles in diameter. As sunlight exerts radiation pressure on the dust particles, they slowly drift away from the coma, forming the comet's bright dust tail.

The gas, meanwhile, dissipates into space. The atoms of gas lose some electrons, and the remaining electrons move to a higher energy level due to the effects of sunlight and vacuum conditions. The resulting gas atoms (ions) that are positively charged are pulled along by the solar wind and fluoresce as the outer remaining electrons fall back to lower energy levels. To remote observers, the fluorescence is visible as a distinct ion tail that is often blue in color and up to a hundred million miles long.

Most comets originate in what is called the Oort Cloud, trillions of miles from our Sun. It is thought to be a nearly spherical shell around the solar system and home to billions or trillions of dormant comets.

NASA's Stardust spacecraft encountered the comet Wild 2 (above) in 2004 and revealed some surprises. Instead of the "dirty snowball" they were expecting, scientists saw a variegated landscape with towering points, tall cliffs, deep craters and numerous jets of particles shooting up from the surface. Some of the pinnacles rose up 330 feet (100m), and some craters were more than 490 feet (150m) deep. Stardust flew right through some of the particle jets, and the spray was so powerful that it damaged the craft's outer shield. Scientists think that what they found on Wild 2 may be typical of other comets.

New comets are usually named for their discoverers, such as Wild 2 after Swiss astronomer Paul Wild. Others, such as Halley, are named for those who calculated their orbits. Still others are named for the observatories or satellites involved in finding them.

COMET WILD 2 (TOP)
CLOSE-UP VIEW HIGHLIGHTS SURFACE FEATURES
VISIBLE-LIGHT IMAGE
STARDUST SPACECRAFT
147 MILES (236KM) FROM STARDUST
2 JANUARY 2004
242 MILLION MILES (389 MILLION KM) FROM EARTH

COMET C/2001 Q4 (NEAT) (LEFT)
VISIBLE-LIGHT COMPOSITE THROUGH RED, GREEN AND BLUE FILTERS
WIYN 0.9M TELESCOPE AT KITT PEAK NATIONAL OBSERVATORY, NOAO
7 MAY 2004
29.7 MILLION MILES (47.9 MILLION KM) FROM EARTH

C

CORONA

The corona, from the Latin word for crown, is the Sun's outermost layer — a roiling, blazing band of hydrogen that extends into space for millions of miles. It is typically visible to the human eye only during a solar eclipse, when it appears like a pearly halo around the edge of the Sun.

Mystery has long surrounded the workings of the corona, especially its intense heat. The corona's temperature of 3,600,000°F (2,000,000°C) greatly exceeds that of the photosphere (10,300°F/5,700°C) and the chromosphere (17,500°F/9,700°C), the two layers that lie under it, closer to the Sun's superheated core (27,000,000°F/15,000,000°C). Why is the corona so hot, when the photosphere (the 250-mile-deep/400km layer of light that we normally see) is actually closer to the Sun's core?

The extreme heat of the corona results from magnetic field lines that rise, threadlike, from the Sun's core as coronal loops. The loops carry energy through the two lower layers without effect — like smoke up a chimney flue. In the corona the loops break and reconnect, releasing charged plasma, which is converted into heat.

The corona itself is composed of three layers: an electron layer containing high-speed electrons; the dust corona, which contains slower-moving particles; and the emission line corona, which emits radiation and ultraviolet light. Because of the corona's intense heat, its protons, neutrons and atomic nuclei move at such phenomenal speeds that many electrons are torn away in the process. As the corona's gases move away from the Sun, they become thinner and cooler, and eventually flow into interplanetary space.

**SOLAR CORONA
AT THE HEIGHT OF
ITS ACTIVITY CYCLE**

LOOP STRUCTURES MAP
OUT MAGNETIC FIELDS

X-RAY IMAGE
(COLOR ADDED)

YOHKOH SPACECRAFT
(EARTH-ORBITING)

1 FEBRUARY 1992

93 MILLION MILES
(150 MILLION KM)
FROM EARTH

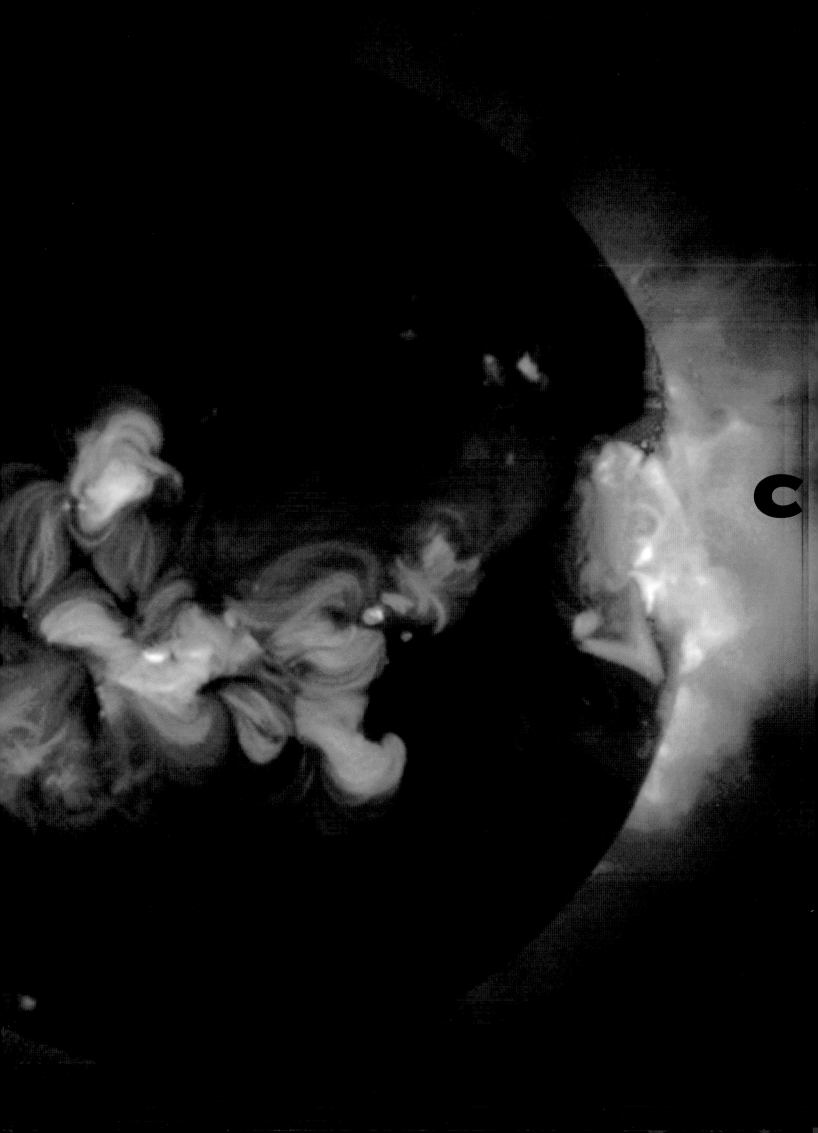

CORONAL LOOP

CORONAL LOOPS ARE MONUMENTAL arches of hot gases that are held in place by a strong magnetic field. The field is formed deep inside the Sun by the chaotic churning of its plasma – gases of charged particles. As the gases move about, the field becomes stronger and more buoyant and starts to rise.

Eventually it balloons through the Sun's surface and becomes visible as coronal loops.

Plasma traces out the loop lines where the magnetic field is most intense. Two sunspots, one of each polarity, might form where these loops appear to perforate the surface. However, what actually happens is

that both the sunspots and the loops are surrounded by an invisible portion of the field. Like magnetic highways, the invisible field constrains the gases to move along it, just as cars travelling on a highway mostly stay in their own lanes.

The loops move through the corona and connect areas of

opposite polarity. They also swing back and forth, responding to the motions of the gas below the surface of the Sun. These motions lead to electrical currents that help heat the corona, just like an old-fashioned radiator heats a room. Sometimes the currents become so large that they can no longer be con-

C

tained by the field, and all hell breaks loose. The field and gas explode in order to eventually reorganize at a lower level of energy. As the field erupts, escaping energy can generate a violent solar flare explosion, and a gigantic plasma cloud, known as a coronal mass ejection, may be released.

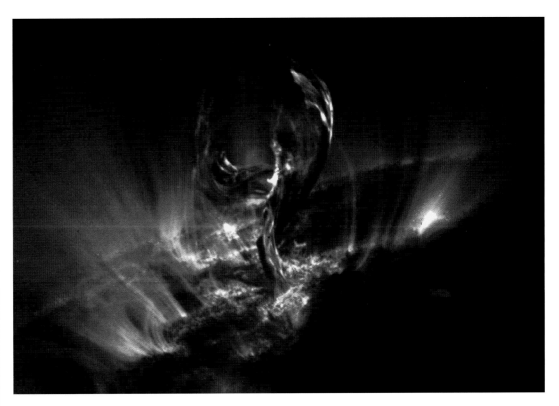

CORONAL MASS EJECTION

CORONAL MASS EJECTIONS (CMEs) are the most dramatic and disruptive of all solar events. Created by the restructuring of magnetic fields, they are big, fast and violent. CMEs are gases of charged particles (plasma) erupting with the solar magnetic field into our Sun's upper atmosphere. And the eruptions are huge. In a matter of hours, they can grow larger than the Sun itself.

Traveling at an average speed of 300 miles (500km) per second, billions of tons of charged particles make up the bulk of a coronal mass ejection. As some of the faster CMEs expand into interplanetary space, they can create shock waves that boost charged particles in the solar wind to velocities near the speed of light.

The impact of a coronal mass ejection is somewhat like a break of billiard balls — energy is transferred from the cue ball to other balls as they're hit and speed across the table. In a CME, charged particles energize more particles in a chain reaction as they accelerate away from the Sun in a particle storm. The results can be disruptive, beautiful or fatal. For example, an astronaut can be in mortal danger if caught unaware in the path of such a storm. And if these charged particles interact with Earth's magnetic field, communications can be disrupted, or colorful light shows known as auroras can be produced in polar skies.

The filamentary structure in the image above is formed by the expansion of a coronal loop system. As the loops heat and rise, a filament lifts off and erupts as a coronal mass ejection. Both hot and cool plasma mixed with radiation are carried out into space. The cooler, heavier particles in the plasma, such as iron, can cause damage to space-based objects. However, if precautions aren't taken, the most serious effects can come from harmful radiation and from the charge buildup generated by the particle storm, which causes electronics to short-circuit.

As with other solar phenomena, such as flares and sunspots, coronal mass ejections have a cycle of about 11 years. During peak periods of magnetic activity, several eruptions can take place in a day.

CORONAL LOOPS (LEFT)
COOLING LOOPS TWO HOURS AFTER A SOLAR FLARE
EXTREME-ULTRAVIOLET IMAGE (COLOR ADDED)
TRACE SATELLITE (EARTH POLAR ORBIT)
19 APRIL 2001
93 MILLION MILES (150 MILLION KM) FROM EARTH

A FILAMENT LIFTS OFF FROM THE SUN AND ERUPTS AS A CORONAL MASS EJECTION (TOP)
THE ENTIRE EARTH COULD EASILY FIT INTO THE ARMS OF THIS 75,000-MILE-HIGH (121,000KM) SOLAR STRUCTURE
EXTREME-ULTRAVIOLET IMAGE (COLOR ADDED)
TRACE SATELLITE (EARTH POLAR ORBIT)
19 JULY 2000
93 MILLION MILES (150 MILLION KM) FROM EARTH

DARK NEBULA

SNAKE NEBULA (BARNARD 72)
THIS LARGE COMPLEX OF GAS
AND DUST BLOCKS THE LIGHT
FROM STARS IN THE BACKGROUND

VISIBLE-LIGHT IMAGE

CANADA-FRANCE-
HAWAII TELESCOPE

2000

500 LIGHT-YEARS FROM EARTH

D

Dark nebulas and reflection nebulas are both gaseous clouds with no internal light source. We see dark nebulas by the absence of light — by the areas of darkness they create as they block light from whatever source lies beyond them. We see reflection nebulas in the starlight that bounces off their particles of dust.

The sinuous form on the left is the Snake Nebula, a chain of clouds that appears in a section of the constellation Ophiuchus. Interstellar dust grains — mostly of carbon — in this dense, dark nebula absorb visible starlight, leaving a snake-shaped stretch of apparent emptiness in the sky.

The emerging light show pictured at right shows the top of the dark Cone Nebula, a giant column seven light-years tall, in a busy star-forming sector of the constellation Monoceros. Radiation from hot young stars in the area has been slowly eroding the nebula for millions of years. The red halo that surrounds the column is caused by the glow of hydrogen gas as it is boiled away by the blistering ultraviolet stellar light.

CONE NEBULA (NGC 2264)
PILLARS OF GAS AND DUST ARE
COMMON IN LARGE STELLAR
NURSERIES. THIS CONICAL SHAPE
IS PROBABLY SCULPTED BY
WIND FROM A NEARBY STAR.

VISIBLE-LIGHT IMAGE

HUBBLE SPACE TELESCOPE
[EARTH-ORBITING]

2 APRIL 2002

2.5 LIGHT-YEARS FROM EARTH

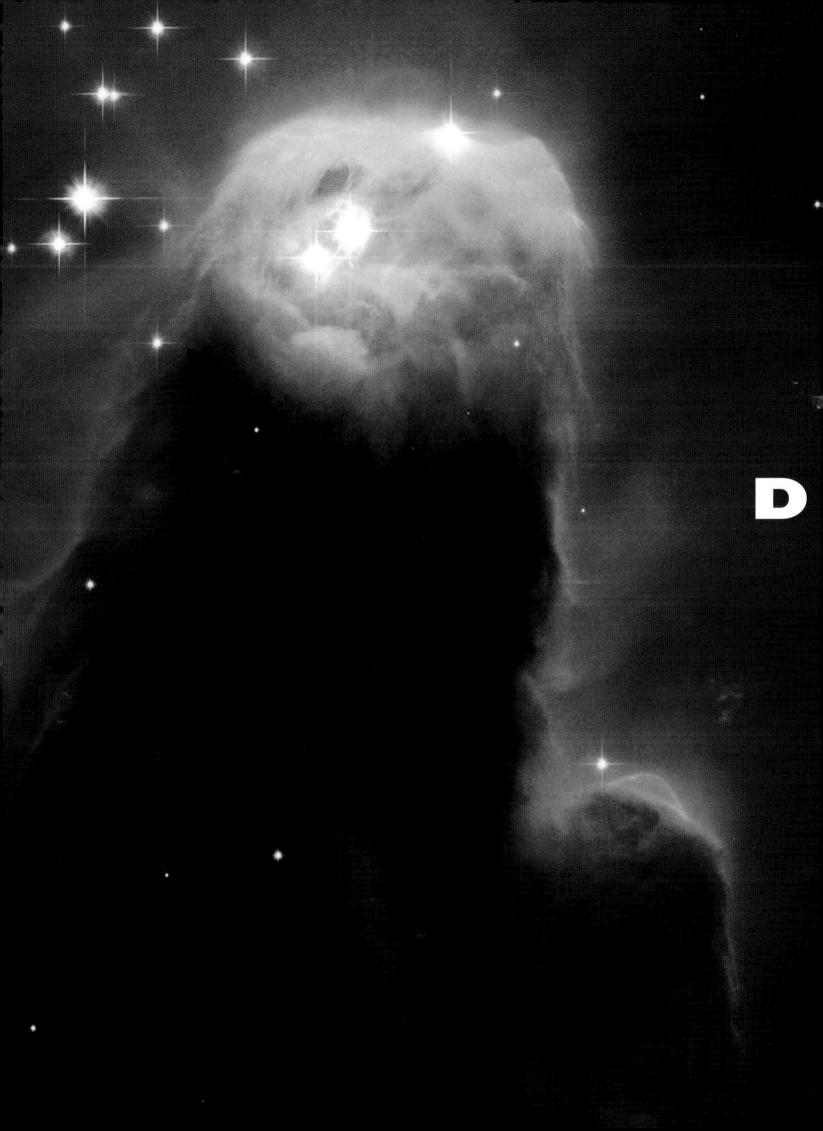

EARTH

THE GREEK WORD FOR LAND IS "ge" or "ga." Gaia was the goddess of the Earth. She was born from the vast emptiness of the universe called Chaos. Viewed from space, Earth distinguishes itself: Set against a black canvas are blue waters, brown-green land masses and white clouds. But what is truly unique about Earth is that as far as astrobiologists can determine, this is the only planet in our solar system where life exists.

Earth is one of nine planets in a solar system located on a spiral arm of the Milky Way Galaxy. It is the third planet from the Sun — an average distance of 93 million miles (150 million km) — and one of the four terrestrial planets in the inner solar system. The fifth largest planet, Earth has one satellite, the Moon.

If Earth is ordinary in size and location, it is extraordinary because of its water and its air. It is the only planet where water exists in abundance and where there is an atmosphere that can support many life forms. Water is the foundation of all life on Earth, and Earth is the only known planet where water exists in all three states: solid, liquid and gas. In liquid form, water covers more than 70 percent of the planet's surface. And even though we know the oceans by names such as the Atlantic and the Pacific, Earth really has just one big ocean.

Powerful forces of wind and water combine to regulate the climate worldwide. They help keep Earth's temperature relatively stable. Winds create daily weather patterns. Oceans have a slower, longer-lasting effect on climate change. The Northern Hemisphere contains most of Earth's land. As a result, it heats and cools quickly, which makes for hotter summers and colder winters. The Southern Hemisphere, by contrast, has more water, which heats and cools more slowly, bringing milder weather with fewer temperature extremes.

E

TRUE-COLOR MOSAIC OF EARTH
TERRA SATELLITE (EARTH-ORBITING)
438 MILES (705KM) FROM TERRA
JUNE–SEPTEMBER 2001

Earth's atmosphere is a layer of gases that surrounds and assists the planet. As a vehicle for our cycle of water, clouds in the atmosphere redistribute water from oceans to land in the form of precipitation. These gases also usefully serve to keep radiation from the Sun both in and out. In a process called the greenhouse effect, gases such as carbon dioxide entrap infrared radiation, thus making the planet warm enough for life to spread. In Earth's upper atmosphere a layer of gaseous ozone (molecules of oxygen with three atoms) acts as a natural sunblock, protecting us from most of the Sun's harmful ultraviolet radiation.

Our atmosphere consists of 78.1 percent nitrogen and 20.9 percent oxygen, the gas we need to breathe. The remaining 1 percent is water vapor and other gases, including carbon dioxide. It is all held together, like almost everything else, by gravity. Ninety-nine percent of the mass of Earth's atmosphere is in the first 40 to 50 miles above the surface. The gases become thinner and thinner with increasing elevation. At about 37,000 miles (60,000km), the atmosphere ends.

High above our atmosphere is a protective shield known as the magnetosphere. Earth is like a huge magnet, which creates our magnetosphere, an invisible magnetic bubble surrounding the planet. The magnetosphere protects Earth by deflecting high-energy ejections from the Sun, which are moving through space at speeds that often exceed a million miles an hour. These ejections of charged particles could destroy life if they all reached Earth's surface. Occasionally some particles break through the magnetosphere and are channeled along invisible lines of force toward the polar regions. When they hit the atmosphere,

they sometimes cause it to glow, creating the famous northern and southern lights.

Earth is the densest body in our solar system. It is made up of several layers: the crust, the upper mantle, the lower mantle, an outer core and an inner core. The crust is a solid layer of rock that forms continents and seabeds. Earth's crust is thinner under the oceans and thicker on land. Most of Earth's mass is contained in its mantles. The upper mantle is hot molten rock, the lower mantle more solid. While Earth's outer core is liquid, the inner core is a solid ball of mostly iron, about the size of Mars. Temperatures at Earth's center are hot — hotter than the Sun's surface.

Earth's surface is young. The crust and upper mantle are broken into seven large and many smaller tectonic plates. Because the upper mantle is hot and moldable, the plates can slide around, spreading apart from and colliding with each other. This shifting causes earthquakes and volcanic eruptions. Most earthquakes occur at the edges of tectonic plates, along fault lines or fractures in the crust. The movement of plates (along with wind and water erosion) reshapes the surface over time; for example, mountains were formed by buckling crust.

Earth is 4.6 billion years old. There are no records of its formative geology or of the organisms that may have lived in the very beginning. We do know that life started in single cells and then multiplied. Scientists have identified about 1.8 million species living today, most of them in the oceans. But the life forms that we see today represent only a small proportion of those that have existed on planet Earth. Over time, most of the species that ever lived — an incredible 99 percent — have died out.

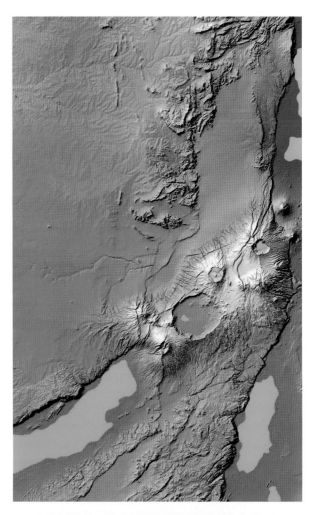

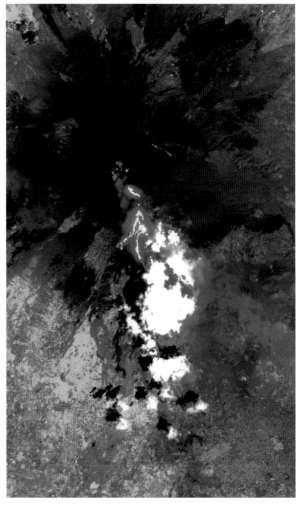

EARTH SCAPES

OLDUVAI GORGE, TANZANIA
(TOP LEFT)

THE GORGE (THE FAINT HORIZONTAL LINE NEAR THE CENTER) IS NOTED FOR EARLY HOMINID FOSSILS

DIGITAL ELEVATION MAP

SHUTTLE RADAR TOPOGRAPHY MISSION

145 MILES (233KM) FROM THE SHUTTLE

11–22 FEBRUARY 2000

RICHAT STRUCTURE, SAHARA DESERT, MAURITANIA
(TOP RIGHT)

THIS DOME OF LAYERED SEDIMENTARY ROCKS IS OFTEN NOTED BY ASTRONAUTS FROM SPACE

LANDSAT IMAGE DRAPED OVER AN ELEVATION MODEL FROM THE SHUTTLE

LANDSAT SATELLITE (EARTH-ORBITING) SHUTTLE RADAR TOPOGRAPHY MISSION

437 MILES (703KM) FROM LANDSAT
145 MILES (233KM) FROM THE SHUTTLE

13 JANUARY 1987 (LANDSAT)
11–22 FEBRUARY 2000 (SHUTTLE)

E

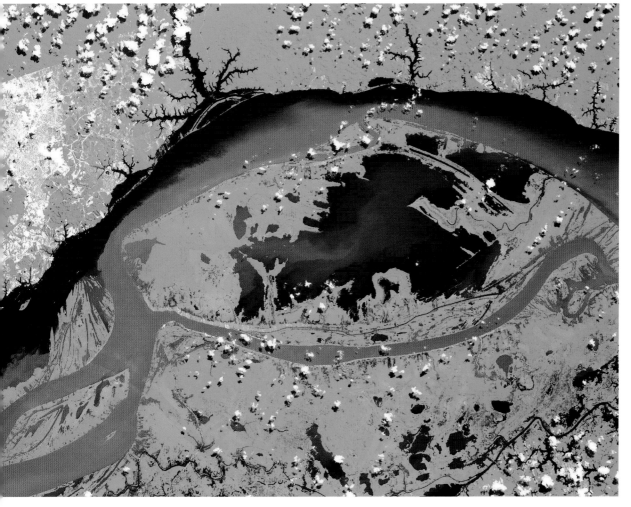

LAVA FLOWS ON THE SOUTHERN FLANK OF MOUNT ETNA
(BOTTOM LEFT)

VISIBLE-LIGHT IMAGE WITH INFRARED LAVA FLOWS

TERRA SATELLITE (EARTH-ORBITING)

438 MILES (705KM) FROM TERRA

29 JULY 2001

JUNCTION OF THE AMAZON AND RIO NEGRO RIVERS AT MANAUS, BRAZIL
(BOTTOM RIGHT)

VISIBLE-LIGHT AND NEAR-INFRARED IMAGE

TERRA SATELLITE (EARTH-ORBITING)

438 MILES (705KM) FROM TERRA

16 JULY 2000

ECLIPSE

On occasion, a celestial body is hidden from view because another body moves in front of it. At other times, a celestial body becomes hidden by the shadow of another. These events are called eclipses.

A solar eclipse occurs when the Moon passes between Earth and Sun and blocks the Sun's light from arriving in some area on Earth. In a total solar eclipse, the entire Sun is blocked out and only a faint halo of light, the corona, is visible. If the Moon covers only part of the Sun, it is called a partial solar eclipse.

When the Earth blocks the Sun's light from the Moon, it is known as a lunar eclipse. A total lunar eclipse occurs when the Moon passes completely through the Earth's shadow. But in a total lunar eclipse, the Moon rarely disappears. Instead, it typically turns red. This results from a small amount of light that reflects off Earth, bends or refracts and then bounces off the Moon. In a partial lunar eclipse, the Moon passes through only a part of the Earth's shadow.

Eclipses are actually happening all the time. In theory, they can be observed anytime and anywhere because they are driven by the location of the observer. For example, if a celestial body passes between you and a star, then you are witnessing an eclipse.

E

**TOTAL ECLIPSE OF
THE SUN BY THE MOON
SHOWS STREAMERS
OF THE SOLAR CORONA**

MOON ILLUMINATED BY
SUNLIGHT REFLECTED
FROM EARTH

COMPOSITE OF 22
VISIBLE-LIGHT IMAGES

FRED ESPENAK WITH
90MM REFRACTING
TELESCOPE

11 AUGUST 1999

238,868 MILES
(384,403KM)
FROM EARTH TO MOON

ECLIPSE
OF THE SUN
BY EARTH

THIS RARE PHOTOGRAPH CAPTURES an eclipse of the Sun by Earth. The phenomenon is unique because it is observable only from space. In this case, the eclipse was recorded by the crew of APOLLO 12 on its return to Earth from the Moon in November 1969. As the trajectory of the spacecraft placed it within Earth's shadow, Earth eclipsed or blocked the Sun.

At the time, the crew members were focused on reentering Earth's atmosphere. So when Mission Control asked them to photograph the passing event, the astronauts had to move quickly to respond. According to Captain Alan Bean, they wasted no time calculating exposures. They bracketed the exposures and "hoped something would turn out." Indeed it did. The astronauts are the only humans ever to have seen, let alone record, an eclipse of the Sun by Earth.

**ECLIPSE OF SUN BY EARTH
AS SEEN FROM SPACE**

VISIBLE-LIGHT IMAGE

HANDHELD 70MM
HASSELBLAD

APOLLO 12

24 NOVEMBER 1969

30,000 MILES (48,000KM)
FROM APOLLO 12 TO EARTH

E

EMISSION NEBULA

THE BRIGHTEST NEBULAS ARE emission nebulas, which generate their own light. In fact, most nebulas we see in the sky are emission nebulas. These are clouds of hot gases, made up mostly of hydrogen. Light from emission nebulas comes from radiation given off by hydrogen atoms. The atoms have been energized by radiation from stars within the nebula or close to it. Most of the visible light seen from emission nebulas is called hydrogen-alpha (H-alpha), a special color of red light produced by warm hydrogen gas.

These stellar nurseries are where newborn stars and stars-in-the-making can be found. The images above show an elongated globule (called the Elephant's Trunk Nebula) within an emission nebula in the constellation Cepheus, 2,450 light-years from Earth. The photograph on the left was taken in visible light. The image on the right was taken by an infrared camera. The infrared image reveals the formation of embryonic stars throughout the Elephant's Trunk Nebula. It also shows clearly the empty area at the head of the globule and the two young stars that have swept up the interstellar matter there.

Elongated globules similar in shape to the Elephant's Trunk Nebula can be seen emanating from the walls of many nebulas. These "elephant trunks" have resisted the photo-evaporating effects of nearby stars and are composed of dense globules of gas and dust, as well as the shielded matter behind them.

On the following pages, the first image shows the Flaming Star Nebula and its illuminating bright blue star, AE Aurigae. Ejected from its birthplace in the neighboring constellation Orion, AE Aurigae zips through space at about 220,000 miles (354,000km) per hour, lighting the Flaming Star Nebula as it passes through, which should take about 10,000 years. After that, the Flaming Star Nebula

E

will no longer be appropriately named, for it will have lost its brilliant glow and will have faded to dark. AE Aurigae's intense radiation causes the nebula's gas to emit hydrogen-alpha light (shown in yellow) and to reflect light (shown in violet), making the Flaming Star both an emission and a reflection nebula.

The final image is the Pelican Nebula, whose clouds of dust and gas are Illuminated by light from massive young energetic stars. The Pelican Nebula, like the Flaming Star Nebula, may also need a name change one day. In millions of years, the strong stellar winds and intense radiation from the young stars will have compressed the gas and dust clouds, creating a new star-and-gas configuration.

ELEPHANT'S TRUNK NEBULA IN VISIBLE LIGHT (LEFT)

DARK GLOBULES SUCH AS THE ELEPHANT TRUNK ARE FEATURES OF LARGE EMISSION NEBULAS

CANADA-FRANCE-HAWAII TELESCOPE

2000

2,450 LIGHT-YEARS FROM EARTH

ELEPHANT'S TRUNK NEBULA IN INFRARED (RIGHT)

THE GLOBULE OF CONDENSED DUST AND GAS IS BUFFETED BY IONIZING RADIATION FROM A NEARBY STAR

SPITZER SPACE TELESCOPE (EARTH-TRAILING SOLAR ORBIT)

5 NOVEMBER 2003

2,450 LIGHT-YEARS FROM EARTH

FLAMING STAR NEBULA (IC 405)

LIT BY AE AURIGAE (CENTER RIGHT), A RUNAWAY BLUE STAR FROM THE CONSTELLATION ORION, THE NEBULA IS BOTH AN EMISSION NEBULA (YELLOW) AND A REFLECTION NEBULA (VIOLET)

VISIBLE-LIGHT COMPOSITE THROUGH 3 FILTERS (REPRESENTATIVE COLOR)

NSF 0.9м TELESCOPE AT KITT PEAK NATIONAL OBSERVATORY, NOAO

21 DECEMBER 1999, 12 JANUARY 2001

1,600 LIGHT-YEARS FROM EARTH

E

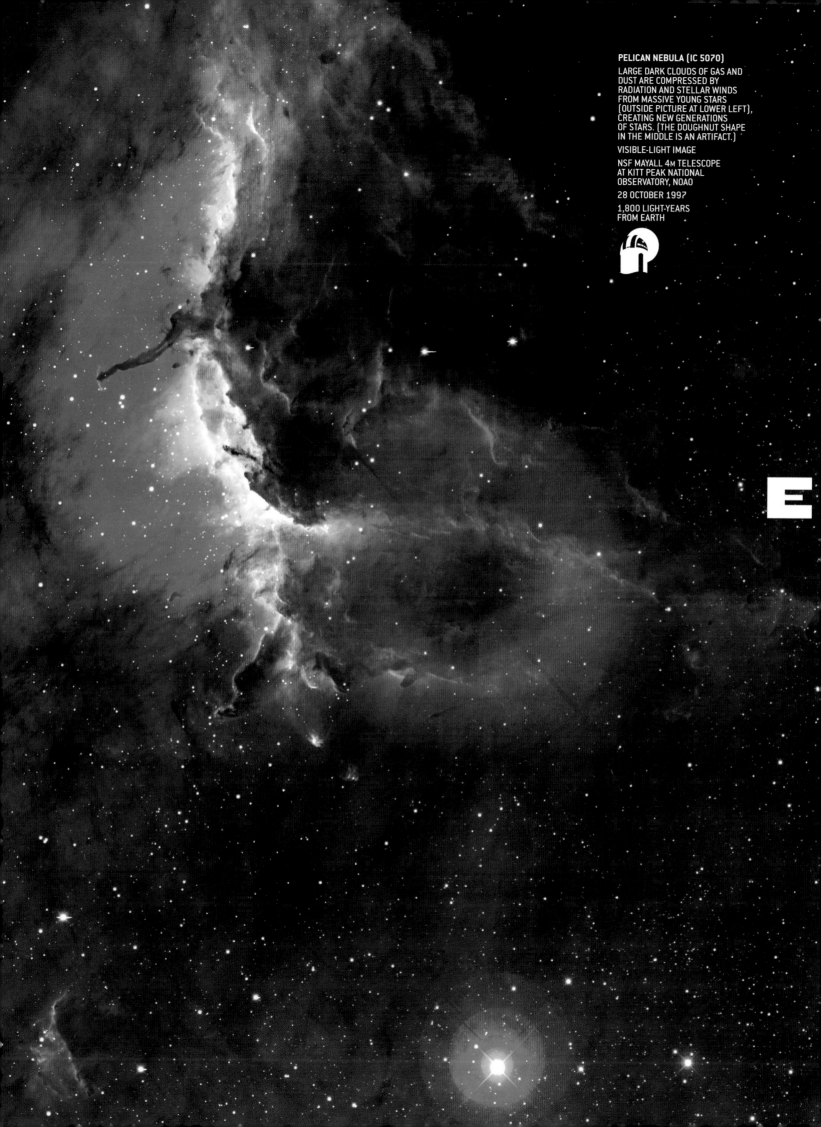

PELICAN NEBULA (IC 5070)

LARGE DARK CLOUDS OF GAS AND
DUST ARE COMPRESSED BY
RADIATION AND STELLAR WINDS
FROM MASSIVE YOUNG STARS
(OUTSIDE PICTURE AT LOWER LEFT),
CREATING NEW GENERATIONS
OF STARS. (THE DOUGHNUT SHAPE
IN THE MIDDLE IS AN ARTIFACT.)

VISIBLE-LIGHT IMAGE

NSF MAYALL 4M TELESCOPE
AT KITT PEAK NATIONAL
OBSERVATORY, NOAO

28 OCTOBER 1997

1,800 LIGHT-YEARS
FROM EARTH

E

EUROPA

In Greek mythology, Europa was a beautiful princess seduced by Zeus, who was disguised as a white bull. The alluring surface of Europa, one of Jupiter's four Galilean moons, is unlike any other in the solar system. It is smooth and beautifully strange, with markings that resemble paint splashed across a palette.

The appearance may have been caused by water, since Europa is largely a ball of it. Some scientists believe that the markings result from global expansion and the moon's crust fractured, filled with water and froze.

E

Liquid water may also exist in Europa's interior. This might be a result of tidal heating initiated by gravitational influences. There is a constant tug of war, in which Jupiter is pulling on one side of the moon while the planet's other major moons are pulling on Europa's other side.

Europa may even have more water than Earth because it possesses a very deep mantle of water. Scientists believe that this water has a high salt content. Europa may have oceans as deep as 31 miles (50km) below its thin crust. The crust is at least three miles (5km) thick and is composed of water and ice.

Despite the tantalizing presence of water, Europa has only a fragile oxygen atmosphere. Sunlight and charged particles hit the icy surface and produce water vapor. Oxygen is released, but not enough to sustain life.

JUPITER'S SATELLITE EUROPA
CRACKS AND RIDGES ON THE FROZEN SURFACE
COMPOSITE IMAGE THROUGH GREEN, VIOLET AND NEAR-INFRARED FILTERS (COLOR ENHANCED)
GALILEO ORBITER
1,300 MILES (2,100KM) FROM GALILEO
1996–1998
417,000 MILES (671,000KM) FROM EUROPA TO JUPITER

E

EUROPA SCAPES

TYPICAL LINEAR DOUBLE
RIDGES SUGGEST
MOLTEN WATER ERUPTIONS
(ABOVE)

VISIBLE-LIGHT MOSAIC
(COLOR ENHANCED)

GALILEO ORBITER

15,000 MILES (25,000KM)
FROM GALILEO

28 JUNE 1996 AND 31 MAY 1998

417,000 MILES (671,000KM)
FROM EUROPA TO JUPITER

IMPACT SCAR THE SIZE
OF HAWAII CAUSED
BY MOUNTAIN-SIZE
ASTEROID OR COMET
(RIGHT)

VISIBLE-LIGHT COMPOSITE
(COLOR ENHANCED)

GALILEO ORBITER

17,900 MILES (29,000KM)
FROM GALILEO

4 APRIL 1997

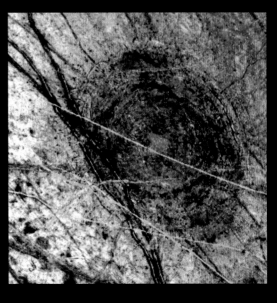

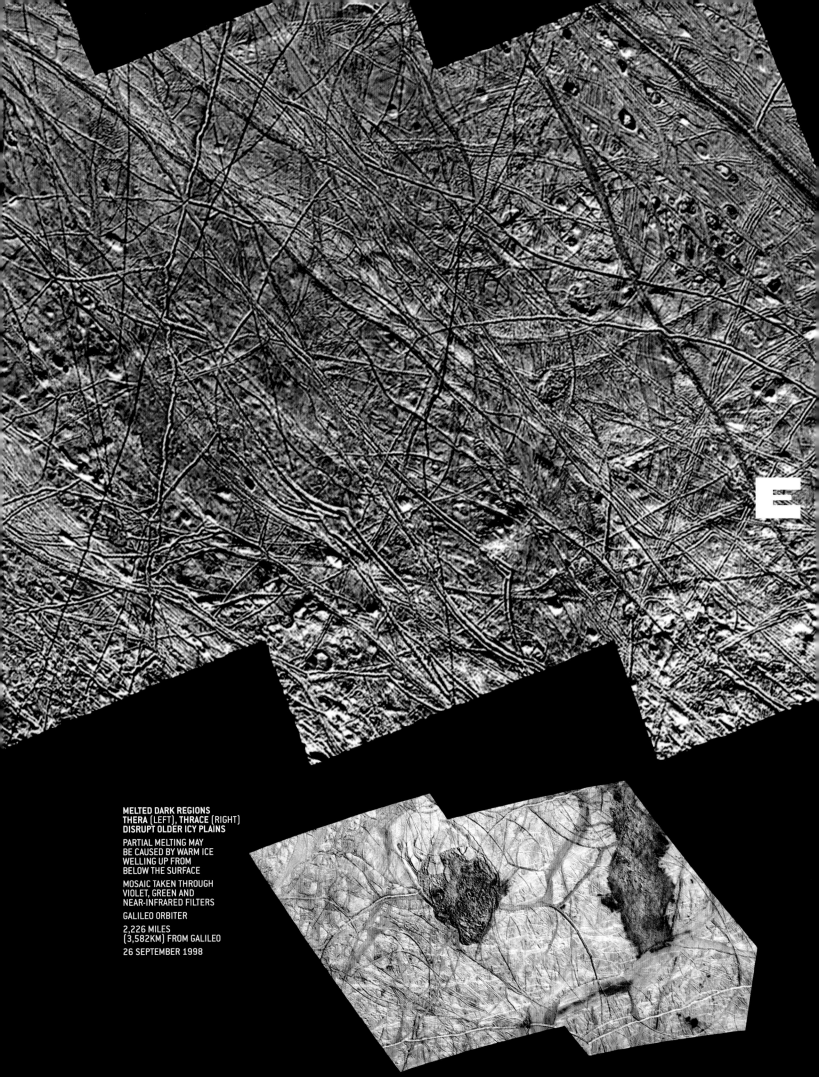

**MELTED DARK REGIONS
THERA** (LEFT), **THRACE** (RIGHT)
DISRUPT OLDER ICY PLAINS

PARTIAL MELTING MAY
BE CAUSED BY WARM ICE
WELLING UP FROM
BELOW THE SURFACE

MOSAIC TAKEN THROUGH
VIOLET, GREEN AND
NEAR-INFRARED FILTERS

GALILEO ORBITER

2,226 MILES
(3,582KM) FROM GALILEO
26 SEPTEMBER 1998

FLARE

FLARES ARE VIOLENT OUTBURSTS of energy and matter that occur around sunspots, causing a sudden radiance. They are the biggest explosions in the solar system. Plasma in the Sun's atmosphere is heated to tens of millions of degrees, and charged hydrogen particles accelerate to near the speed of light. Flares emit radiation and shock waves that can last from minutes to hours.

Scientists theorize that flares are released when the Sun's magnetic field lines tear and reconnect, expelling a large amount of magnetic energy into the corona. According to Dr Brian R. Dennis, astrophysicist at the Goddard Space Flight Center, the largest solar flares are energetically equivalent to 100 billion times the size of the atomic bomb dropped on Hiroshima.

Flares follow the solar cycle of magnetic activity that spans an 11-year period of high and low intensities. When the cycle is at its peak, flares increase in frequency and force.

Flares and coronal mass ejections (CMEs) often occur together, suggesting there may be a connection. But while the energized particles from flares tend to be confined to the solar vicinity, the CME particles – moving away from the Sun at near the speed of light – go off into interplanetary space.

CMEs are believed to be the main source of high-energy charged particles that pose dangers to astronauts traveling to the Moon or Mars. But the relationship between flares and CMEs is not fully understood. Considerable research is under way due to safety concerns about the impact of these gigantic solar events on future space projects.

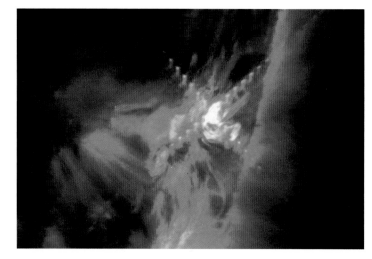

SOLAR FLARE WITH ERUPTIONS SPRAYING MATERIAL FROM NORTHWEST TO SOUTHWEST

THE MULTIPLE BRIGHT POINTS IN THE CROSS SHAPE ARE EFFECTS CAUSED BY THE INTENSE BRIGHTNESS OF THE FLARE

EXTREME-ULTRAVIOLET IMAGE (COLOR ADDED)

TRACE SATELLITE (EARTH POLAR ORBIT)

16 MAY 1999

93 MILLION MILES (150 MILLION KM) FROM EARTH

FLARE

THE WHITE HORIZONTAL LINE IS AN ABERRATION CAUSED BY THE INTENSE BRIGHTNESS OF THE FLARE

EXTREME-ULTRAVIOLET IMAGE (COLOR ADDED)

EIT TELESCOPE ON SOHO SPACECRAFT

92 MILLION MILES (148 MILLION KM) FROM SOHO

4 NOVEMBER 1997

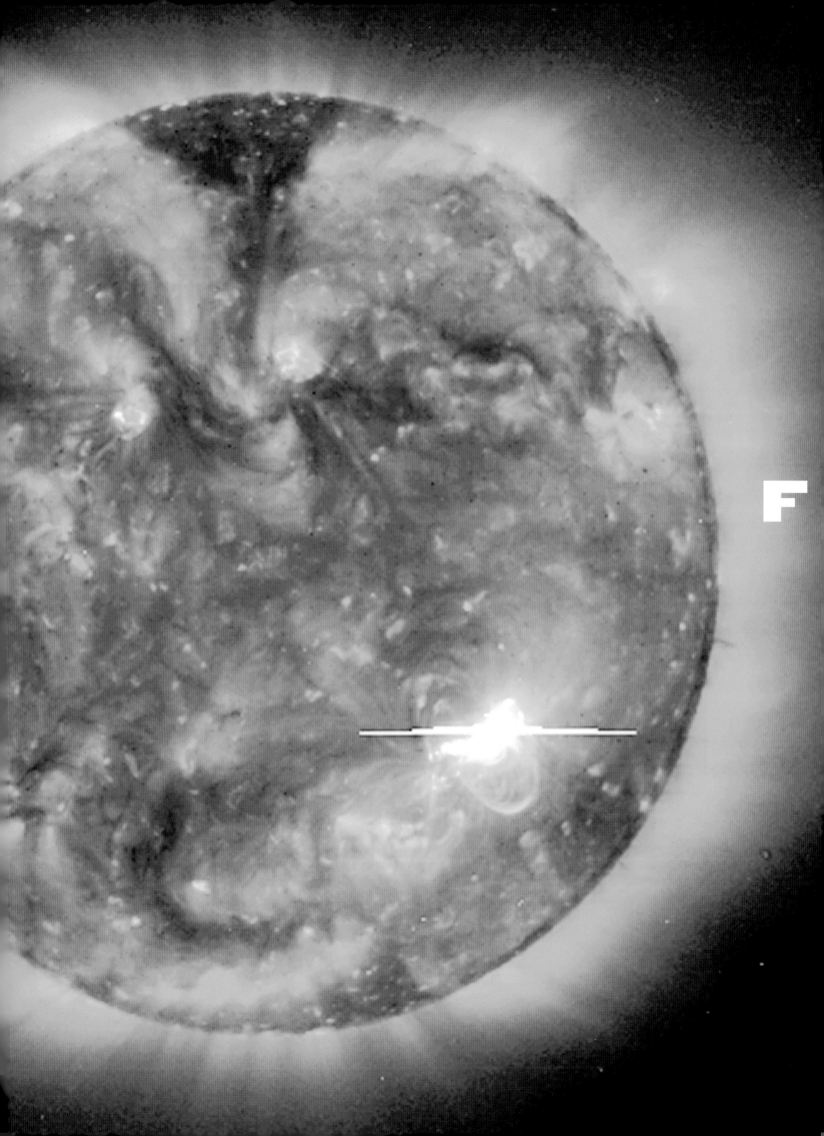

GALACTIC CENTER

In the direction of the con-stellation Sagittarius, about 25,000 light-years away from Earth, millions of stars are huddled together in the galactic center of the Milky Way.

The outermost region of the center, 500 light-years wide, is known as the bulge. In the large image, the bulge is visible at lower left, glowing behind a mottled foreground of dust. The strong point of light within the glow is the inner core — a dense mass of stars 30 light-years wide. The inner core can be seen in the close-up above. Hidden in the clouds is a three-armed feature called the Mini-Spiral, which surrounds our central supermassive black hole.

This black hole, known as Sagittarius A* (pronounced A star), is the geometric center of our galaxy. It weighs in at three million times the mass of our Sun and its event horizon spans some 24 million miles (39 million km). Black holes at the center of galaxies have huge appetites. They binge on inter-stellar gas and dust and emit radiation. The emissions from Sagittarius A* are comparatively weak, suggesting that explosive events have cleared away its gaseous supply of food.

G

THE SUPERMASSIVE BLACK HOLE SAGITTARIUS A* IS AT THE CORE OF THE MILKY WAY (TOP)

X-RAY IMAGE

CHANDRA X-RAY OBSERVATORY (EARTH-ORBITING)

21 SEPTEMBER 1999– 4 JUNE 2002

25,000 LIGHT-YEARS FROM EARTH

THE GALACTIC CENTER OF THE MILKY WAY GALAXY IN THE CONSTELLATION SAGITTARIUS (LEFT)

THE BULGE IN THE REGION AT LOWER LEFT HARBORS THE BLACK HOLE

INFRARED COMPOSITE IMAGE REVEALS OTHERWISE HIDDEN STARS

2MASS (EARTH-BASED)

APRIL 1997, MARCH 2001

25,000 LIGHT-YEARS FROM EARTH

G

GALAXY

A GALAXY IS A GIGANTIC GROUPING of stars, a kind of metropolis. Like all cities, galaxies evolve over time. They are fluid structures in a constant state of change.

Gravity pulls together the dark and luminous matter that fills interstellar space to create galaxies. Gravity holds them together and also brings them together. They collide and merge, which is usually how galaxies grow. And it is because of gravity that galaxies congregate in galactic clusters. The Milky Way is just one of about three dozen galaxies in a cluster known as the Local Group.

G

Galaxies come in a huge assortment of sizes. Jumbo galaxies can have as many as 3,000 billion stars, as well as other stars-in-the-making. Even the smallest galaxies are likely to have approximately 200,000 stars. Our own galaxy, the Milky Way, holds between 100 billion and 200 billion.

There are three basic galactic forms. Elliptical galaxies are shaped more or less like oval balls. They are also the largest. Spiral galaxies, such as our own Milky Way, typically have a bulging center and slender, curving arms in a disk. Irregular galaxies, which have no defined shape, are usually small and have relatively few stars.

In his classification of galaxies, Edwin Hubble said that spirals evolved from ellipticals. Scientists now believe that it is the other way around: Spirals merged to form ellipticals.

SOMBRERO GALAXY (M 104) IN THE VIRGO CLUSTER

NEARLY EDGE-ON VIEW, 50,000 LIGHT-YEARS ACROSS

VISIBLE-LIGHT MOSAIC

HUBBLE SPACE TELESCOPE (EARTH-ORBITING)

MAY–JUNE 2003

28 MILLION LIGHT-YEARS FROM EARTH

DWARF GALAXY

THE BEST MODEL FOR THE BIRTH of galaxies in the early universe predicts an invisible form of matter known only by its gravitational force. Because this matter is missing light, it is called dark matter. Not long after the Big Bang, dark matter was able to attract ordinary matter in the form of vast clouds of gas. The thickest clouds contracted to form stars and galaxies. Dwarf galaxies were the first to emerge.

Because the newborn galaxies were small, gravity was low. Matter could escape and merge with other matter, seeding the universe with dwarf galaxies. These then grew by clumping together to form larger galaxies, or were digested by large galaxies that grew by cannibalizing small ones. Modern galactic structures such as spirals and ellipticals descended from these diminutive forebears.

Dwarf galaxies are typically irregular in shape, some more spherical than others. It is thought that the earliest dwarf was a flat disk. As the primordial disk continually merged with other infant galaxies, the flat structure of stars was tossed around, becoming more spheroidal. Both varieties are still common today. The Milky Way has about a dozen dwarf satellite galaxies. These survivors did not get caught up in typical galactic mergers. One of the satellites, Sagittarius Dwarf Irregular (above), is spheroidal. It is dim and spread out because it is slowly being stretched apart by the Milky Way's irresistible gravity.

SPIRAL GALAXY

SPIRAL GALAXIES ARE THE MOST ubiquitous cities of stars in the universe. They are broad, flattened disks of stars, dust and gas, distinguished by long, curving, blue-white arms that wind around a bright central bulge of older stars. Until a century ago, they were thought of as "spiral nebulas" around nearby newborn stars. But they were simply too far away for individual stars to be resolved without a large telescope.

Within these starry pancakes there is an ongoing "galactic ecology" where stellar debris is recycled into successive generations of stars. Galactic disks would be largely

G

indistinguishable from each other were it not for density waves (analogous to ripples on a pond). The wave action is thought to create the spiral arms, where gas and dust pile up and ignite into firestorms of star birth. Computer simulations show that the arms are dynamic and can re-form in other regions of the disk. If the arms did not change, over time they would wind up tightly, like a watch spring, as the galaxy rotates. But they do not. This complex and not fully understood process makes each spiral galaxy as unique as individual snowflakes.

Spiral galaxies were created from the merger of smaller galaxies in the early universe. By the time the universe was half its present age, the spirals were fully formed. But the evolution has not ended. When spiral galaxies merge, they create elliptical galaxies as the stars are scattered out of the plane of the disks. In our galactic neighborhood, the Milky Way is the second largest spiral after the Andromeda Galaxy, 2.2 million light-years away. The two spirals are speeding toward each other at 300,000 miles (483,000km) per hour. In several billion years they may collide and form one enormous elliptical galaxy.

BARRED SPIRAL GALAXY

A PROMINENT BARLIKE FEATURE is thought to appear in roughly one-third of spiral galaxies. In fact, the Milky Way has a recently discovered small bar. This galactic type is identified by the presence of stars and interstellar matter along a bar in the central bulge, with spiral arms swirling from the ends.

One current theory is that most barred spirals result from interactions with nearby galaxies, which set up instabilities in the spiral disk. The encounter gravitationally rearranges the rotation of some stars from circular orbits to more elliptical ones. These stars trace out the barlike pattern. They also rob momentum from gas in the disk so that it flows toward the center of the galaxy along the bar. Shock waves prevent clouds from collapsing and forming new stars in the bar.

In the Milky Way, the bar is relatively short. Scientists know it is there by measuring the velocities of hydrogen, which respond to the gravity of the stars, and by measuring starlight in infrared, which sees through interstellar pollution.

A galaxy possibly similar to the Milky Way is the barred spiral galaxy NGC 7424, at left. Both are in the intermediate class of galaxies between normal spirals and those that are strongly barred, and both are about 100,000 light-years across. Surrounding the radiant golden bar of NGC 7424 are bluish-gray winding arms, studded with red dots. The bluish hues indicate the presence of massive young stars and the reddish dots signify areas of star formation.

ELLIPTICAL GALAXY

AS AGEING SPIRAL GALAXIES engulf and devour each other, the injured disks lose their shape, scattering the orbits of stars, almost like a swarm of bees. The newly configured structure swells into a star-studded sphere known as an elliptical galaxy.

Ellipticals are like gigantic cotton balls in the sky. Their 3-D shape can range from nearly round to oval. Since they do not have enough dust or gas to sustain star formation, ellipticals are usually yellow-red in color due to their older star population, compared with the blue cast of spirals with younger stars. Elliptical galaxies are common among large, crowded galaxy clusters, supporting the theory that they form through mergers and collisions.

NGC 1316 in the constellation Fornax (above) looks like a typical elliptical galaxy, but it is caught in the act of swallowing a smaller disk galaxy. Traces of spiral arms and a disk are evidence that the fusion is not yet complete.

G

THE BARRED SPIRAL GALAXY NGC 7424 IN THE CONSTELLATION GRUS (LEFT)

NGC 7424 BELONGS TO AN INTERMEDIATE CLASS OF GALAXIES BETWEEN NORMAL SPIRALS AND THOSE STRONGLY BARRED

VISIBLE-LIGHT COMPOSITE

EUROPEAN SOUTHERN OBSERVATORY VIMOS + 8.2M VLT MELIPAL TELESCOPE

9 OCTOBER 2004

40 MILLION LIGHT-YEARS FROM EARTH

THE GIANT ELLIPTICAL GALAXY NGC 1316 IN THE CONSTELLATION FORNAX (TOP)

VEINED DUST LANES SHOW THAT NGC 1316 IS MERGING WITH A SPIRAL GALAXY

VISIBLE-LIGHT IMAGE

EUROPEAN SOUTHERN OBSERVATORY VLT ANTU + FORS 1

9–19 JANUARY 2000

50 MILLION LIGHT-YEARS FROM EARTH

SEYFERT GALAXY

A SEYFERT GALAXY IS A SPECIAL spiral galaxy with an energetic center. This compact and active core, or nucleus, releases bright clouds and filaments. Excited matter is propelled by a superwind created by a supermassive black hole. Seyfert galaxies are part of a class of objects called Active Galactic Nuclei (AGN). These have the ability to blow gas from their cores at high speed due to active central black holes.

In the photographs, the central fountainlike shape is a bubble of gas being blown by winds released in a burst of star formation. In the close-up above, four streams of gaseous filaments shoot above the disk at more than four million miles (six million km) an hour. The gas whirls around in a vortex and is expelled into space. Eventually, gas will rain down on the galaxy's disk, where it may collide with gas clouds, compress them and form new stars. Many astronomers think that all spirals erupt now and then. Our own Milky Way may once have been or will be a Seyfert galaxy.

IRREGULAR GALAXY

G

AN IRREGULAR GALAXY IS WHAT IT sounds like – disorganized. It does not have a distinct spiral or elliptical shape. Irregular galaxies are grouped by their independent nature because they don't fit anywhere else.

Sometimes irregulars exist in isolation and sometimes they are formed by collisions, near misses and gravitational forces as they interact with other galaxies. Irregulars are smaller than spiral or elliptical galaxies. Most are low-mass galaxies composed of millions, not billions, of stars.

From the Southern Hemisphere, two prime irregular galaxies can be spotted with the unaided eye – the Large and Small Magellanic Clouds. These two satellite galaxies are gravitationally bound to the Milky Way and are being stretched by the attraction of the larger galaxy.

The irregular dwarf galaxy above is located in the constellation Sagittarius in the Milky Way's Local Group. With a heavy population of hot, massive blue stars, Barnard's Galaxy is located in our neighborhood, just 1.6 million light-years away. The gas bubble in the top right corner is a cocoon of stars born in the gas cloud. Spirited stellar winds from the baby stars pushed the extra gas from the cloud into space, where it expands without interference or interruption.

BARNARD'S GALAXY (NGC 6822), A DWARF IRREGULAR GALAXY IN THE CONSTELLATION SAGITTARIUS
VISIBLE-LIGHT IMAGE
(REPRESENTATIVE COLOR)
NSF BLANCO 4M TELESCOPE AT
CERRO TOLOLO INTER-AMERICAN
OBSERVATORY, NOAO
1, 2 SEPTEMBER 2000
1.6 MILLION LIGHT-YEARS
FROM EARTH

THE SEYFERT GALAXY NGC 3079 (RIGHT) **AND A CLOSE-UP OF ITS CORE** (ABOVE)
VISIBLE-LIGHT IMAGE
HUBBLE SPACE TELESCOPE
(EARTH-ORBITING)
26 NOVEMBER 1998
50 MILLION LIGHT-YEARS
FROM EARTH

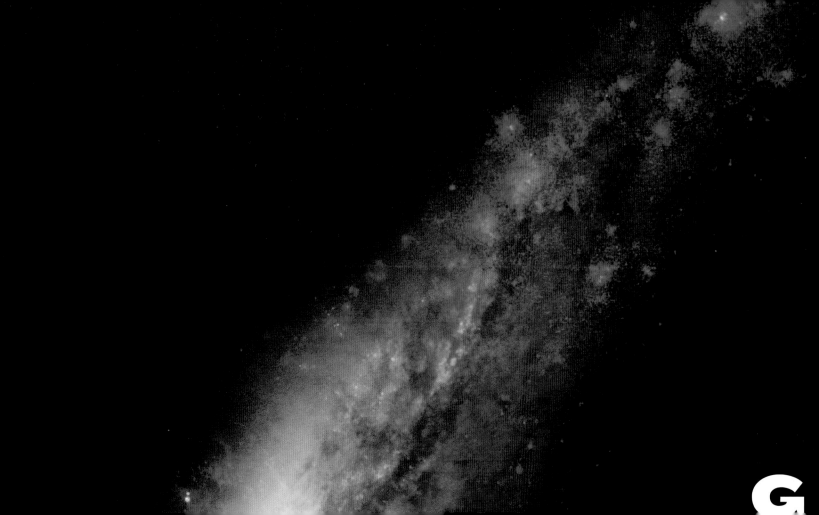

STARBURST GALAXY

A STARBURST GALAXY IS A BRIEF but vivid firestorm of star birth. For about 10 million years – a relatively short burst in the life of a 10-billion-year-old galaxy – star formation occurs at hundreds of times the rate it does in normal galaxies. The young stars are big and bright, so starbursts stand out as the most luminous galaxies in the sky.

The high birth rate is probably spawned by a close encounter or collision with another galaxy. Shock waves cause giant clouds of gas and dust to collapse and form stars. The young stars burn out quickly because they are so massive, and they explode as supernovas. A chain reaction of shock waves and star formation drives through the galactic center, where most of the gas is located. The burst of activity stops once most of the gas has been used up or blown away.

In our local universe, starburst galaxies are rare now, but they were more common billions of years ago. All galaxies were closer together then, so they were more likely to bump into one another. More frequent encounters produced more starbursts as galactic forms evolved with the expanding universe.

LENTICULAR GALAXY

WHEN VIEWED EDGE ON, LENTICU-lars are shaped like a double-convex lens. When viewed face on, they resemble elliptical galaxies, which are more spherical. Lenticulars look like a transitional stage between spirals and ellipticals. The rotund appearance, however, probably has a different origin. Lenticulars could be spiral galaxies with the arms wound tight – so tight around the center that they have disappeared into an accentuated bulge and bulbous shape.

In lenticular galaxy NGC 2787 (above), evidence of the vanishing arms is visible in the concentric rings of swirling dust around the bright nucleus.

THE STARBURST GALAXY M 82
(LEFT)
A SUPERGALACTIC WIND BLOWS LEFT AND RIGHT FROM A NEARLY VERTICAL DISK OF STARS
COLOR-CODED VISIBLE-LIGHT COMPOSITE
WIYN 3.5M TELESCOPE AT KITT PEAK NATIONAL OBSERVATORY, NOAO, WITH DATA FROM THE HUBBLE SPACE TELESCOPE
SEPTEMBER 1997,
MARCH 1997, AUGUST 1998,
DECEMBER 2001
12 MILLION LIGHT-YEARS FROM EARTH

THE LENTICULAR GALAXY NGC 2787
(ABOVE)
VISIBLE-LIGHT IMAGE
HUBBLE SPACE TELESCOPE (EARTH-ORBITING)
29 JANUARY 1999
24 MILLION LIGHT-YEARS FROM EARTH

G

WARPED GALAXY

A GALAXY LIKE THE MILKY WAY is basically a thin, flat disk, but its outer regions are slightly warped, almost like the brim of a hat, bending down on one side and up on the other. This warping is now known to be common in spiral galaxies.

Far more pronounced warping is shown in the gently undulating disk above, an edge-on view of galaxy ESO 510-G13 in the constellation Hydra.

The large spiral is in the process of digesting a smaller galaxy with which it has collided, causing distortion of the disk by gravitational forces. The twisted structure is illuminated by the central bulge. Eventually, after the merger settles down, the spiral galaxy will become more regular in appearance. ESO 510-G13 was first seen in photographs taken by the European Southern Observatory.

RING GALAXY

IN THE RARE RING GALAXY, ONE galaxy travels right through the disk of another, drastically altering its form. The gravitational shock of the impact compresses gas into a ring, where new stars are born. In the ring at right, an "intruder" galaxy has passed through a normal spiral, catapulting elements of the "target" galaxy into a necklace of blue star clusters around the nucleus.

AN EDGE-ON VIEW OF THE WARPED GALAXY ESO 510-G13
THE TWISTED DISK STRUCTURE INDICATES A RECENT COLLISION WITH A NEARBY GALAXY
VISIBLE-LIGHT IMAGE
HUBBLE SPACE TELESCOPE (EARTH-ORBITING)
6–7 APRIL 2001
150 MILLION LIGHT-YEARS FROM EARTH

THE RING GALAXY AM 0644-741
VISIBLE-LIGHT IMAGE
HUBBLE SPACE TELESCOPE (EARTH-ORBITING)
16–17 JANUARY 2004
300 MILLION LIGHT-YEARS FROM EARTH

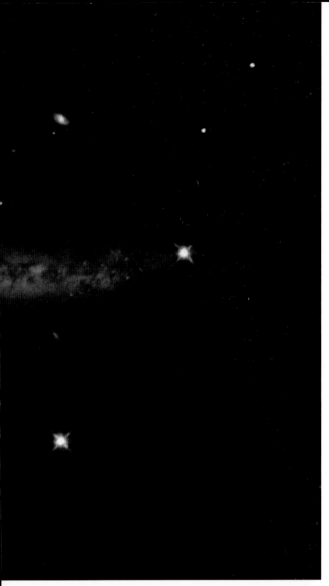

G

BACKWARD SPIRAL GALAXY

A BACKWARD SPIRAL GETS ITS name from its outer arms of gas and stars, which lead in the direction of the galaxy's rotation. In most spirals, such as the Milky Way, these density lanes trail behind the direction of rotation, as if following in its wake. The backward spiral here also has a quirky inner arm, which is rotating in the opposite direction. The likely explanation is that NGC 4622 was disturbed by a smaller galaxy, which it is in the process of incorporating.

THE BACKWARD SPIRAL GALAXY NGC 4622

VISIBLE-LIGHT COMPOSITE

HUBBLE SPACE TELESCOPE (EARTH-ORBITING)

25 MAY 2001

111 MILLION LIGHT-YEARS FROM EARTH

GANYMEDE

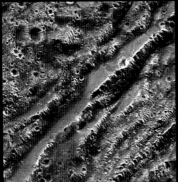

THE LARGEST OF JUPITER'S MOONS, Ganymede is the largest satellite in our solar system. If Jupiter can be compared to the hub of a great city, then Ganymede is the biggest building on the block. In fact, if Ganymede orbited the Sun, its size, basic composition of rock and ice and magnetic field would probably qualify it as a planet. It is 3,270 miles (5,262km) wide, larger than the planet Mercury.

Named for the youth who was cupbearer to the Olympian gods, Ganymede is made of a mostly rocky core, a water and ice mantle, and a crust of rock and ice. The satellite has what is considered a complex geological history, with mountains, valleys, craters and lava flow.

Ganymede's surface is covered by dark and light regions. The dark regions are heavily cratered, suggesting they are very old. The brighter regions are believed to have been formed more recently, possibly by tectonic tension (the shifting of plates that compose the surface). These light regions have ridges and grooves that create a complex pattern, with formations that range from a few hundred to thousands of miles.

Although Ganymede has no substantial atmosphere, the Hubble Space Telescope detected a small amount of surface ozone. Scientists suspect that the ozone is produced by charged particles in Jupiter's magnetic field that rain down and mix with the icy surface, causing water in the ice to begin ozone production. The ozone suggests that Ganymede may have a thin and fragile oxygen atmosphere similar to that of its sister satellite Europa.

GANYMEDE'S STAIR-STEP CLIFFS MAY HAVE BEEN FORMED BY TECTONIC FAULTING
VISIBLE-LIGHT IMAGE
GALILEO ORBITER
1,200 MILES (2,100KM) FROM GALILEO
20 MAY 2000
665,000 MILES (1,100,000KM) FROM GANYMEDE TO JUPITER

G

JUPITER'S SATELLITE GANYMEDE
VISIBLE-LIGHT MOSAIC (COLOR ENHANCED)
VOYAGER 2
186,000 MILES (300,000KM) FROM VOYAGER 2
26 JUNE 1996
665,000 MILES (1,100,000KM) TO JUPITER

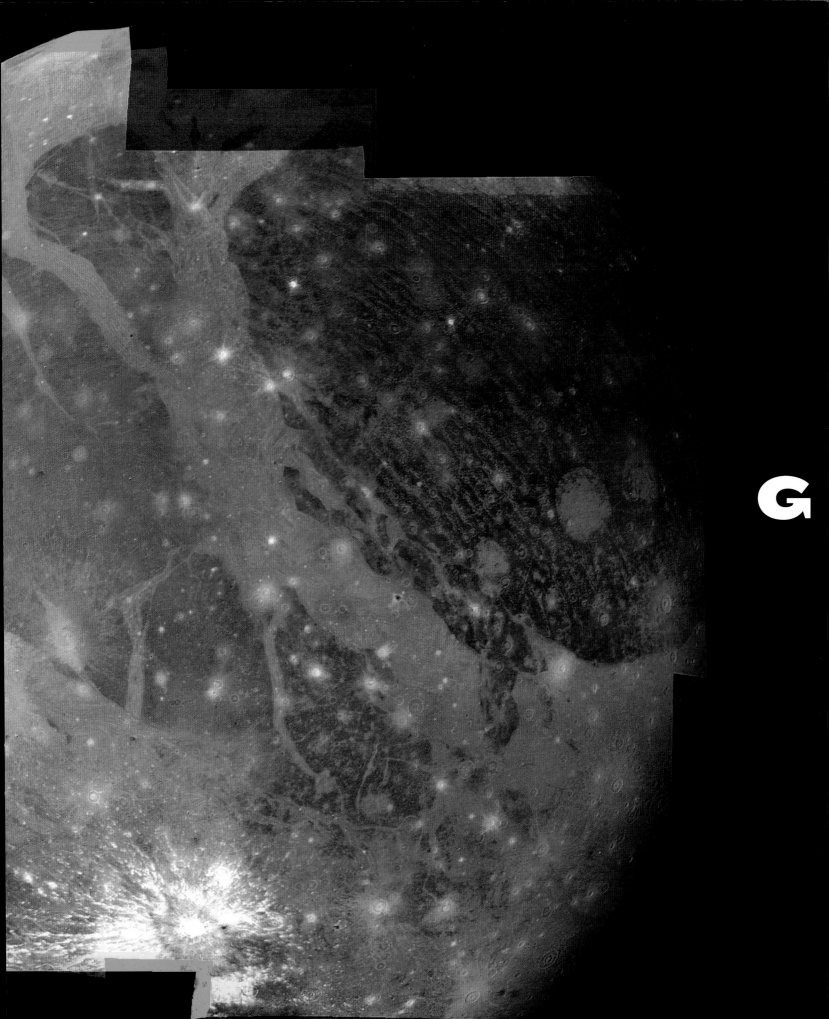

G

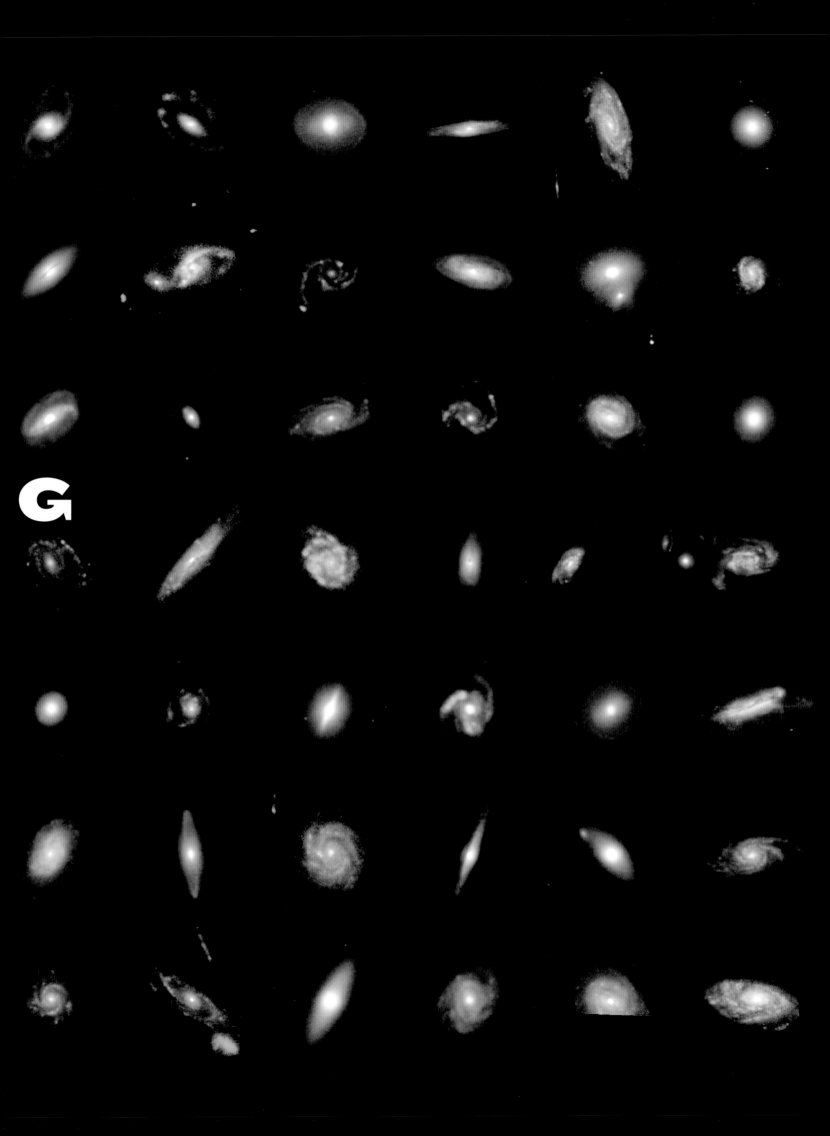

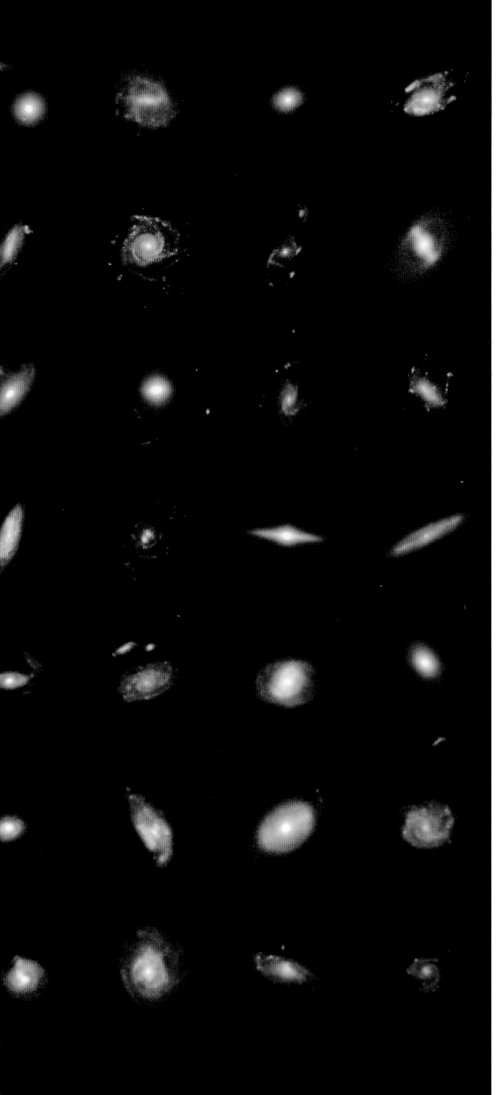

GEMS SURVEY

THIS COLLECTION OF GALACTIC jewels, a mosaic of 70 images, is a tool for studying the formation of the universe. The images were taken from a much larger photograph, the GEMS Survey. That remarkable composite image of 40,000 galaxies in the constellation Fornax was pieced together from 78 separate exposures taken by the Hubble Space Telescope's Advanced Camera for Surveys. Even though the GEMS photograph is the largest color image Hubble has ever produced, it covers only a small piece of the sky — about the size of an aspirin tablet held at arm's length.

The survey (GEMS is an acronym for Galaxy Evolution from Morphology and SEDs, or Spectral Energy Distributions) seeks to determine the relative age, evolution and relationships of the galaxies that make up the universe. Images of the most distant galaxies allow scientists to see back in time some nine billion years. Among the questions they hope to answer is how gravitational forces affect the formation, merger and evolution of galaxies. They are also studying the role of stellar bars, concentrations of stars that affect the course of galaxy formation by pushing gas toward the galactic center, which sometimes results in the birth of new stars.

GEMS SURVEY

GALAXY EVOLUTION FROM MORPHOLOGY AND SPECTRAL ENERGY DISTRIBUTIONS

VISIBLE-LIGHT MOSAIC OF SELECT GALAXIES FROM THE SURVEY

HUBBLE SPACE TELESCOPE OPERATED BY THE SPACE TELESCOPE SCIENCE INSTITUTE; OBSERVING PROGRAM: MAX-PLANCK-INSTITUTE FOR ASTRONOMY

AUGUST 2002–MARCH 2003

100 MILLION–10 BILLION LIGHT-YEARS FROM EARTH

GLOBULE

WHEN NEBULAS PRODUCE NEW stars, the process starts with a lump within a huge, dark, cold cloud of hydrogen known as a globule. Some disturbance — perhaps an exploding supernova — sets things in motion. The globule contracts under the force of gravity. It becomes so dense and hot in the core that it triggers nuclear reactions which generate enough heat to stop the collapse — and a star is born.

Globules come in a number of shapes and sizes. There are huge globules, stretching for tens of light-years, and smaller globules that look like black bubbles when seen against a starry background or a glowing nebula. The globules at right, in a major star-forming region of the constellation Centaurus, were spotted by astronomer A.D. Thackeray in 1950. They stand out clearly against brightly lit gas and dust that has been heated by massive stars far hotter than our Sun.

Emerging from the walls of some nebulas are long, slender columns known as "elephant trunks." These phantasmagoric shapes, such as the Horsehead Nebula, are created when the blistering ultraviolet light from a nearby star boils away nebular gas. Dense globules can resist this photoevaporation, shielding matter directly behind them. The globule and the dust-laced gas behind it form the elephant trunk.

THACKERAY'S GLOBULES IN THE ACTIVE STAR-FORMING REGION IC 2944

EACH GIANT GLOBULE IS 1.4 LIGHT-YEARS ACROSS

VISIBLE-LIGHT IMAGE

HUBBLE SPACE TELESCOPE (EARTH-ORBITING)

FEBRUARY 1999

5,900 LIGHT-YEARS FROM EARTH

GRAVITATIONAL LENS

Imagine that you were suspended in Earth's atmosphere and could look through a giant magnifying glass at the surface below. In space, there are natural occurrences that act as a magnifier or zoom lens. This phenomenon, called a gravitational lens, is a massive object, such as a large galaxy or galaxy cluster, that bends and magnifies the light of galaxies located far behind it.

But how does a gravitational lens work? How does it actually bend the light? Although light travels in a straight line, the direction is influenced by space. Most of the matter in space is dark matter, an invisible form that is the source of most gravity in the universe. The gravity of dark matter holds galaxy clusters together. According to Einstein's theory of general relativity, gravity warps and bends space, distorting a beam of light. So when light passes through the gravitational lens formed by a galaxy cluster, the light is distorted and bent. Although Einstein predicted the effects of gravity on light in space, he thought it would be difficult to observe them from Earth.

Science has known about gravitational lenses since the 1970s, but the Hubble Space Telescope has brought them into fine detail. The Hubble has used a gravitational lens to get a view of the distant universe by looking through the galaxy cluster known as Abell 1689, located 2.2 billion light-years away. Hubble astronomers have speculated that some of the objects in view are more than 13 billion light-years away.

The use of gravitational zoom lenses, like other cutting-edge explorations into what's out there, lets us see farther into the universe. And in a wonderful cosmic twist, the farther we see into space, the farther back in time we go.

THE CENTER OF GALAXY CLUSTER ABELL 1689 IS A GIANT MAGNIFYING GLASS IN SPACE

THIS GRAVITATIONAL LENS ENLARGES GALAXIES BILLIONS OF LIGHT-YEARS AWAY

VISIBLE-LIGHT IMAGE

HUBBLE SPACE TELESCOPE (EARTH-ORBITING)

JUNE 2002

2.2 BILLION LIGHT-YEARS FROM EARTH

HYDROGEN SKY

HYDROGEN IS ALL AROUND US. The primordial element has been the main component of the universe since the Big Bang. This all-sky hydrogen survey maps the distribution of hydrogen atoms across the entire Milky Way Galaxy.

"Hydrogen makes up the atmosphere of galaxies," says Dr Jay Lockman of the National Radio Astronomy Observatory at Green Bank, West Virginia. This atmosphere, or interstellar medium, is both the source of clouds that create new stars and the repository of gas outflow from existing stars. The atmosphere is much more extensive than the visible Milky Way.

It governs the future of our galaxy by determining where new stars will form and what their composition will be.

A neutral hydrogen atom is made up of a proton and an electron, each of which spins like a top on its axis. In its lowest energy state, the particles spin in opposite directions. But occasionally the atom will collide with another, flipping the electron's spin to a higher energy state. After a few million years, the electron will spontaneously flip back. When it does, it emits a radio wave. Although this process is extremely slow, there are so many hydrogen atoms in the Milky Way that their collec-

ALL-SKY HYDROGEN MAP, WITH THE PLANE OF THE MILKY WAY GALAXY RUNNING THROUGH THE CENTER

RADIO IMAGE (COLOR ADDED)

NATIONAL RADIO ASTRONOMY OBSERVATORY, GREEN BANK

PARKES RADIO OBSERVATORY

BELL LABORATORIES, CRAWFORD HILL

UNIVERSITY OF CALIFORNIA AT BERKELEY, HAT CREEK

1970S–1980S

A FEW LIGHT-YEARS TO 100,000 LIGHT-YEARS FROM EARTH

tive radio signal is easily detected on modern radio telescopes.

The presence of hydrogen is most intense along the galactic plane (color coded in red). The high density of hydrogen can lead to the creation of new stars, for a star like our Sun is mostly hydrogen. It is estimated that one star a year is formed from

the clouds of hydrogen in the Milky Way. At the other end of the star cycle, the wavelike cloud structures (above, left of center) show evidence of massive clusters of stars gone supernova.

The continuing study of neutral hydrogen could be important in locating dark matter. Scientists measuring the velocity of

hydrogen far from the galactic plane found that it is gravitationally bound to a large amount of matter. This mysterious matter was originally called missing mass; but the mass was not missing, because the hydrogen reacted to its gravitational tug. What was missing was its light – hence the name dark matter.

INFRARED CIRRUS

To THE NAKED EYE, VAST STRETCH-es of sky appear dark and empty – a velvet backdrop against which the movements of planets and stars can be read. But space is not empty. The infrared cirrus is found in nearly every direction. A surprise discovery in the late 20th century was that the "invisible void" is filled with wispy clouds of gas – mostly hydrogen and helium – and dust. The fine particulate dust is mainly made of carbon, silicon and oxygen.

The amorphous structures have been named infrared cirrus because they resemble the cirrus clouds in Earth's atmosphere and can be detected only through infrared light. A mixture of intense cold and slight heat

is the reason infrared cirrus can be seen only in this wavelength. It is a cosmic deep freeze with temperatures as low as −400 °F (−240 °C). Only a little bit of warmth, provided by visible and ultraviolet light from nearby stars, is efficiently absorbed by the dust. The dust re-radiates the absorbed energy, which can be seen only in infrared.

The emissions of infrared cirrus help scientists understand the structure of our galaxy. The current consensus is that the Milky Way is a barred spiral galaxy. The bar has a strong concentration of gas and dust that provides most of the emission we see in the above image. The density of this interstellar substance

varies throughout space. It can be dispersed in a supernova blast. It can be blown about by interstellar winds. And it can gather together in more crowded areas called nebulas. Infrared cirrus is the recycling material of stars — both the residue of stellar explosions and the raw ingredients that form new stars.

INFRARED CIRRUS

THE "EMPTY AREAS" BETWEEN STARS ARE FILLED WITH DUST THAT CANNOT BE SEEN IN VISIBLE LIGHT

INFRARED IMAGE

MSX SATELLITE (NEAR SUN-SYNCHRONOUS ORBIT)

24 APRIL 1996–20 FEBRUARY 1997

15,000–18,000 LIGHT-YEARS FROM EARTH

IO

According to myth, Io was a young woman changed into a cow by Zeus to protect her from his wife's jealous rage. It didn't work. Hera recognized the girl and sent a gadfly to torment her. Io was left wandering throughout the Mediterranean. The satellite Io has been described as tormented too – but as a result of ongoing volcanic activity. Spewing from Io's violent vents, toxic concoctions, primarily of sulfur, continually spray paint the surface red, yellow and white.

Io is Jupiter's third largest moon and a little larger than our own. It is situated closest to Jupiter and is the innermost of the planet's four Galilean moons. Io has an iron core that takes up half its diameter, which means it could possibly have its own magnetic field. Auroras have been documented on Io by the Cassini spacecraft, resulting from an electric current running between the moon and Jupiter.

Io is the most volcanically active body in our solar system. The crust of the satellite is being constantly flexed due to the gravitational interplay between Jupiter and the moons Europa and Ganymede. For every four times Io goes around Jupiter, Europa goes around twice and Ganymede once. This phenomenon, known as orbital resonance, forces the normally circular orbits of these moons to follow more oblong paths. Because the distance between the satellites and Jupiter is constantly changing, the force of gravity on Io increases and decreases.

Just as a rubber ball can be heated by repeated squeezing and releasing, Io is heated by such gravitational flexing. This keeps the subsurface hot and drives Io's volcanic activity.

JUPITER'S SATELLITE IO

ASTRONOMERS NICKNAMED IO THE "PIZZA MOON" AFTER ITS WHITE, YELLOW, RED AND BLACK COLORATION. THE DIFFERENT COLORS REPRESENT SULFUR OR SULFUR COMPOUNDS FORMED AT DIFFERENT TEMPERATURES.

VISIBLE-LIGHT IMAGE (COLOR ENHANCED)

GALILEO ORBITER

310,000 MILES (500,000KM) FROM GALILEO

19 SEPTEMBER 1997

263,000 MILES (424,000KM) FROM IO TO JUPITER

IO: PELE ERUPTING

MOST OF IO'S VOLCANOES, LIKE Pele, are saucer-shaped, lacking the high peaks of shield volcanoes such as Mauna Loa and Mauna Kea on Earth. Classified as "paterae" (from the Latin for shallow dish), more than 400 scar Io's terrain, but only a few produce plumes.

Pele's umbrella-shaped dust plume can arch to a few hundred miles, but its giant form is faint against the surface and is easiest to see against the dark backdrop of interplanetary space. The source of Pele's dust plume appears to be a churning underground lava lake that regularly reveals its hot contents and raises sulfur-

Most dust plumes are smaller and denser than Pele's. The smaller variety appear blue in daylight, contrasting with the warm hues of Io's landscape. Frosts deposited on the surface by these smaller plumes are thought to be responsible for resurfacing much of the moon.

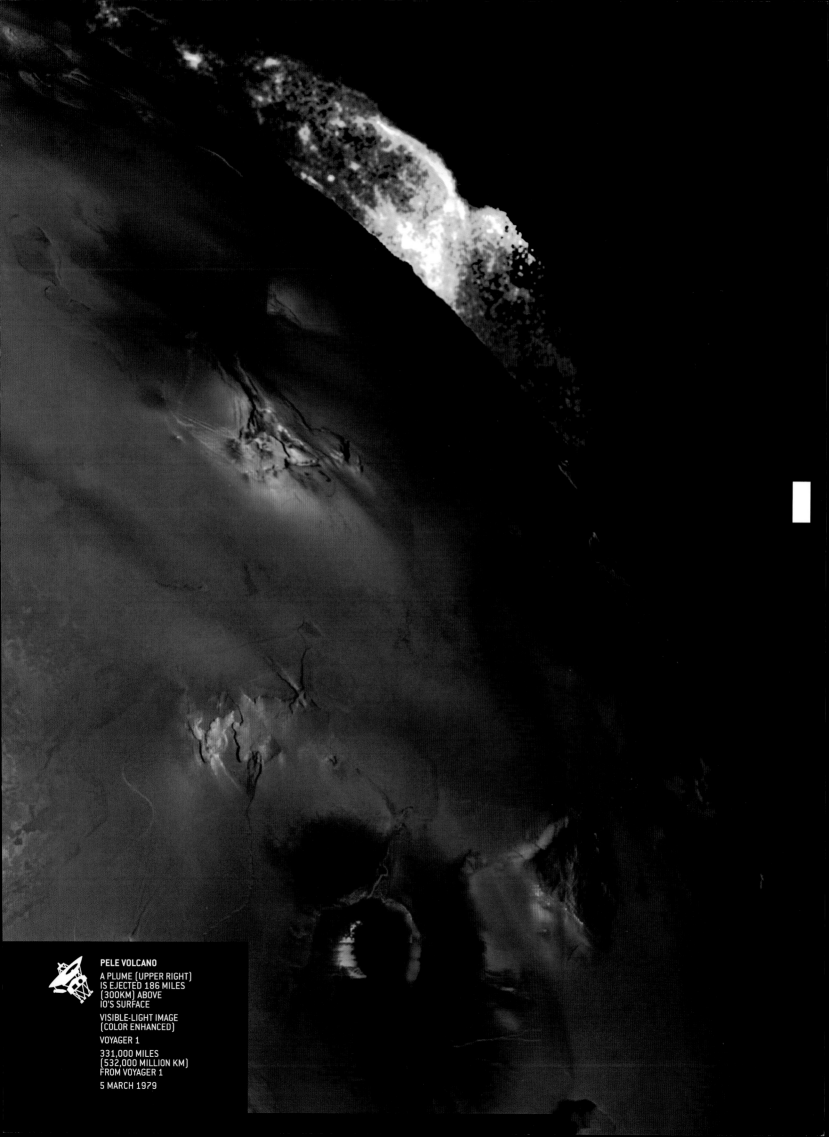

PELE VOLCANO

A PLUME (UPPER RIGHT)
IS EJECTED 186 MILES
(300KM) ABOVE
IO'S SURFACE

VISIBLE-LIGHT IMAGE
(COLOR ENHANCED)

VOYAGER 1

331,000 MILES
(532,000 MILLION KM)
FROM VOYAGER 1

5 MARCH 1979

IO:
CAPTURED
BY A GIANT

AMONG ALL THE JOVIAN MOONS, Io has the strongest link with its mother planet. It's a complex relationship formed by Io's volcanic gases and Jupiter's powerful magnetic field. The bond takes shape as a halo.

Here's how it works. Neutral atoms of oxygen and sulfur gases are thrown into space by Io's volcanoes. The atoms become ionized by the Sun or by Jupiter's radiation belt. The ions (charged particles) around Io stick to invisible lines of intensity in Jupiter's magnetic field. The magnetic field moves in synchronization with Jupiter's rotation. As the magnetic field sweeps by Io, it drags with it ionized gas in circular paths, forming a doughnut-shaped halo called a torus around the planet. What begins as a sphere of charged particles encompassing Io is molded into a halo surrounding Jupiter. Wherever the torus passes through Jupiter's shadow, the faint glow becomes visible.

Meanwhile, as Io orbits Jupiter ensconced in the planet's torus, an intense stream of electrons flows along the planet's magnetic field lines, connecting Io to Jupiter at any given moment. Known as the Io flux tube, this electrical connection between the two bodies travels around the planet with Io, instead of with Jupiter's much faster magnetic field. The flux tube permits periodic radio transmissions from a naturally generated Jovian source and is considered to be the largest electric circuit in the solar system.

THE SATELLITE IO IN ORBIT AROUND JUPITER

VISIBLE-LIGHT IMAGE

CASSINI ORBITER

6.2 MILLION MILES (9.9 MILLION KM) FROM CASSINI TO JUPITER

1 JANUARY 2001

262,000 MILES (422,000KM) FROM IO TO JUPITER

JUPITER

NAMED AFTER THE ROMAN GOD OF all gods, Jupiter is the largest planet in the solar system. Second in brightness after Venus as viewed from Earth, Jupiter could be filled with a thousand Earths. Yet it measures only one-tenth of the Sun's diameter.

The planet is like a bustling metropolis, with many satellites, a colorful ring system, turbulent storms and streaks of lightning. Like the hub of a great city – Times Square in New York or the Ginza in Tokyo – Jupiter is big, bright and commanding.

In 1610, Galileo discovered Jupiter's four largest moons – Io, Europa, Ganymede and Callisto – now called the Galilean satellites. Today we know that Jupiter has at least 63 satellites – the most of any planet in the solar system. Scientists speculate that many of the outer moons may be asteroids caught by the planet's intense gravity.

Jupiter is one of the four gas giants, along with Saturn, Neptune and Uranus. In composition, Jupiter is similar to a star. In fact, the gas giant sends out into space more than one-and-a-half times the heat it receives from the Sun. Yet, even with all the right stuff, Jupiter falls short of the weight require-

ment for a star to ignite. The planet needs about 80 times more mass for fusion to commence in its core.

Even though Jupiter has no solid surface, its designation as a gas giant is strangely misleading. The majority of the planet is made of hydrogen under such supersize pressure that it has turned liquid and metallic. Jupiter is divided into four main layers: a thin outer envelope of gaseous hydrogen, a deep sea of liquid hydrogen, a deeper sea of liquid hydrogen acting like molten metal and a hot core of ice and rock.

Jupiter has a strong magnetic field generated by electrical currents deep in the planet's liquid metallic hydrogen layer. Within the magnetic field there is an abundance of charged particles. These particles create dangerous radiation, which bombards Jupiter's rings and moons. The planet's strong magnetic field interacts with the solar wind to create a magnetic tail that extends as far as Saturn's orbit.

JUPITER
A TRUE-COLOR MOSAIC
OF 27 IMAGES
CASSINI ORBITER
6.2 MILLION MILES
(10 MILLION KM)
FROM CASSINI
29 DECEMBER 2000
391 MILLION MILES
(629 MILLION KM)
FROM EARTH

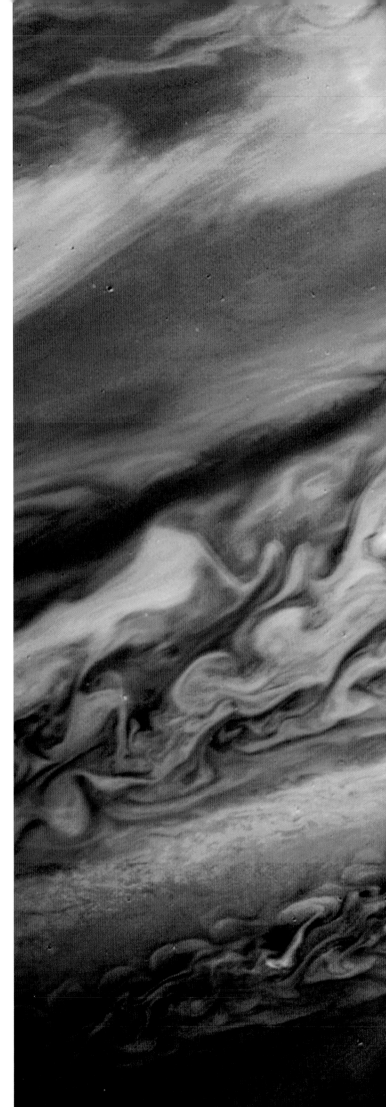

JUPITER'S GREAT RED SPOT

JUPITER'S MOST NOTABLE feature may be its Great Red Spot, a huge storm system more than 12,500 miles (20,000km) wide, or about twice the width of Earth. It is, in fact, the largest storm in our solar system. And it has been there, in Jupiter's southern hemisphere, for at least 350 years, since English naturalist Robert Hooke first reported it. But it is now only half as big as it was a century ago.

The Great Red Spot is a vortex of high and cool clouds driven by strong winds of up to 250mph (400kph). Scrunched in between two jet streams in the upper atmosphere, the mass of clouds twirl upward and rotate counterclockwise every six days. It is anticyclonic — that is, a high-pressure system, unlike the low-pressure cyclonic hurricanes on Earth. Storms like this one last so long on the gas giants because there are no solid surfaces below to break them up.

Along with smaller cloud systems that act like thunderstorms, the Great Red Spot is located in Jupiter's kaleidoscopic cloud lanes. As pictured on the previous spread, the lighter bands are rising gases called zones, while the darker bands are descending gases called belts. Perpetual strong winds, steady alternating jet streams and the fast rotation of the planet (a day is under ten hours) — all contribute to these atmospheric stripes.

JUPITER'S GREAT RED SPOT
VISIBLE-LIGHT IMAGE
VOYAGER 2
3.7 MILLION MILES (6 MILLION KM) FROM VOYAGER 2
3 JULY 1979
500 MILLION MILES (805 MILLION KM) FROM EARTH

J

JUPITER: THE RINGS

Jupiter's ring system (the horizontal lines in the photograph) was first discovered in 1979 by NASA's Voyager 1 spacecraft. We now know that the planet's ring is made up of three major sections.

The main ring, approximately 4,000 miles (6,500km) wide, is encircled by the orbits of two small moons, Adrastea and Metis. Its inner border merges into the faint and thickest ring, called the halo. This doughnut shape extends halfway from the main ring to Jupiter's cloud tops and may be caused by the electrical charging of particles that spiral inward. Neighboring the main ring on the outside is a pair of faint gossamer rings. One of the pair is contained by the orbit of the moon Amalthea and the other by the moon Thebe. The gossamers are thicker than the main ring due to the inclined path of the two moons as they circle Jupiter.

The Jovian ring system is highly tenuous and uniform, composed of tiny dust particles a few microns in diameter. Astronomers speculate that the rings may be formed by dust kicked up as interplanetary meteoroids smash into the planet's inner moons — Metis, Adrastea, Amalthea and Thebe.

RING SYSTEM TO THE LEFT AND RIGHT OF A BACKLIT JUPITER

COMPOSITE OF TWO MOSAICS IN VISIBLE LIGHT

RINGS: GALILEO ORBITER ARCS OUTLINING JUPITER: VOYAGER 2

1.4 MILLION MILES (2.3 MILLION KM) FROM GALILEO

RINGS: 9 NOVEMBER 1996 ARCS: 1979

500 MILLION MILES (805 MILLION KM) FROM EARTH

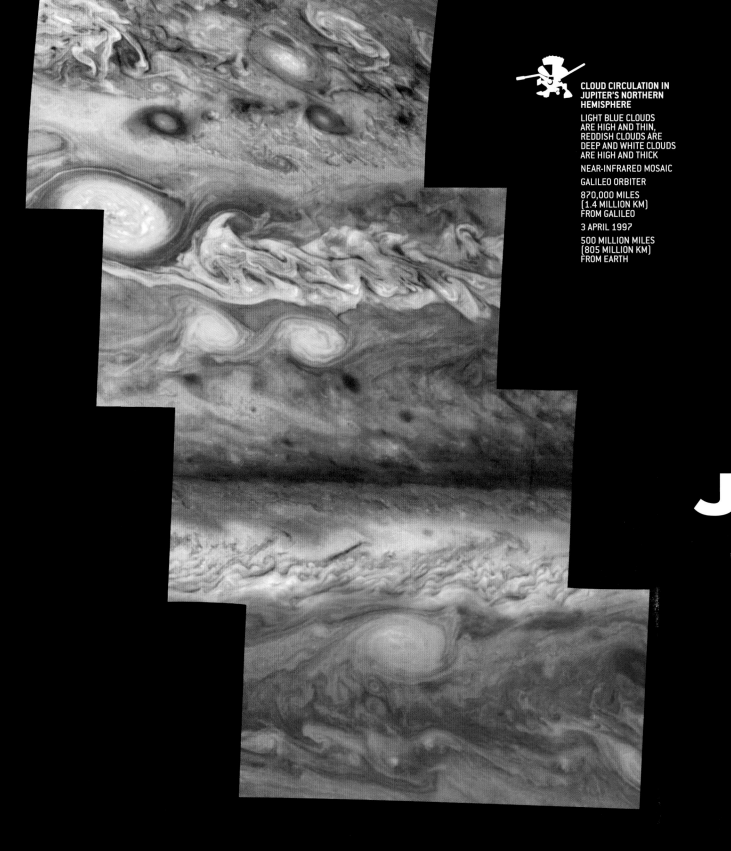

CLOUD CIRCULATION IN JUPITER'S NORTHERN HEMISPHERE

LIGHT BLUE CLOUDS ARE HIGH AND THIN, REDDISH CLOUDS ARE DEEP AND WHITE CLOUDS ARE HIGH AND THICK

NEAR-INFRARED MOSAIC

GALILEO ORBITER

870,000 MILES (1.4 MILLION KM) FROM GALILEO

3 APRIL 1997

500 MILLION MILES (805 MILLION KM) FROM EARTH

J

THE CLOUDS

MUCH LIKE A STAR, JUPITER'S gaseous atmosphere is about 90 percent hydrogen and 10 percent helium. Floating above the gases is the visible cloud layer. Composed of ammonia (NH_3) ice crystals, the colorful shell is many miles thick and very turbulent, with no solid surface beneath. The clouds result from hotter temperatures at lower altitudes causing ammonia to well up from the interior. As the ammonia rises into colder and higher altitudes, it freezes and forms the clouds. The billowing marbled coloration is probably caused by chemical contaminants.

Giant lightning flashes have been detected by both the Voyager and Galileo probes. The lightning occurs in anticyclonic regions where turbulence is formed by abruptly changing winds traveling from north to south. The source of these electrical discharges may be water-ice clouds located at a lower altitude.

LIGHT ECHO

WHEN A NOVA FLARES OR A supernova explodes, there is a brilliant flash of light. There is also an echo – a light echo – as the initial burst of brilliance is reflected in the neighboring dust and interstellar clouds. Over time, as the echo travels out from the star, it appears to form an expanding ring, covering a larger and larger area. This ring of light is constantly changing as it reaches and illuminates additional layers of material.

Light echoes are rare sightings. But in January 2002 a relatively dim star suddenly flared, becoming 600,000 times brighter than our Sun – temporarily the brightest star in the Milky Way.

This sequence of photographs was taken by the Hubble Space Telescope over a two-year period. They seem to show a cloud of dust expanding into space faster than the speed of light. But the cloud is not moving. What we are seeing is more and more of the surrounding cloud as it becomes illuminated by the traveling starlight. Before the Hubble's recording, the last sighting of a light echo in the Milky Way was in 1936.

A LIGHT ECHO FROM THE STAR MONOCEROTIS (V 838) IN THE CONSTELLATION MONOCEROS

A HALO OF LIGHT APPEARS TO EXPAND AROUND A RED GIANT EXPLOSION

VISIBLE-LIGHT IMAGE

HUBBLE SPACE TELESCOPE (EARTH-ORBITING)

30 APRIL 2002– 23 OCTOBER 2004

20,000 LIGHT-YEARS FROM EARTH

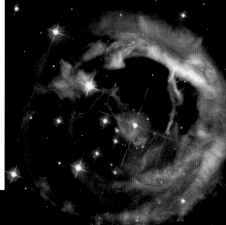

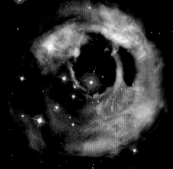

COMPUTER-GENERATED
SPHERE MADE FROM 24
VISIBLE-LIGHT IMAGES

MARS GLOBAL
SURVEYOR ORBITER

230 MILES (370KM)
FROM THE ORBITER
(AVERAGE)

10–11 APRIL 1999

62 MILLION MILES
(100 MILLION KM)
FROM EARTH

M

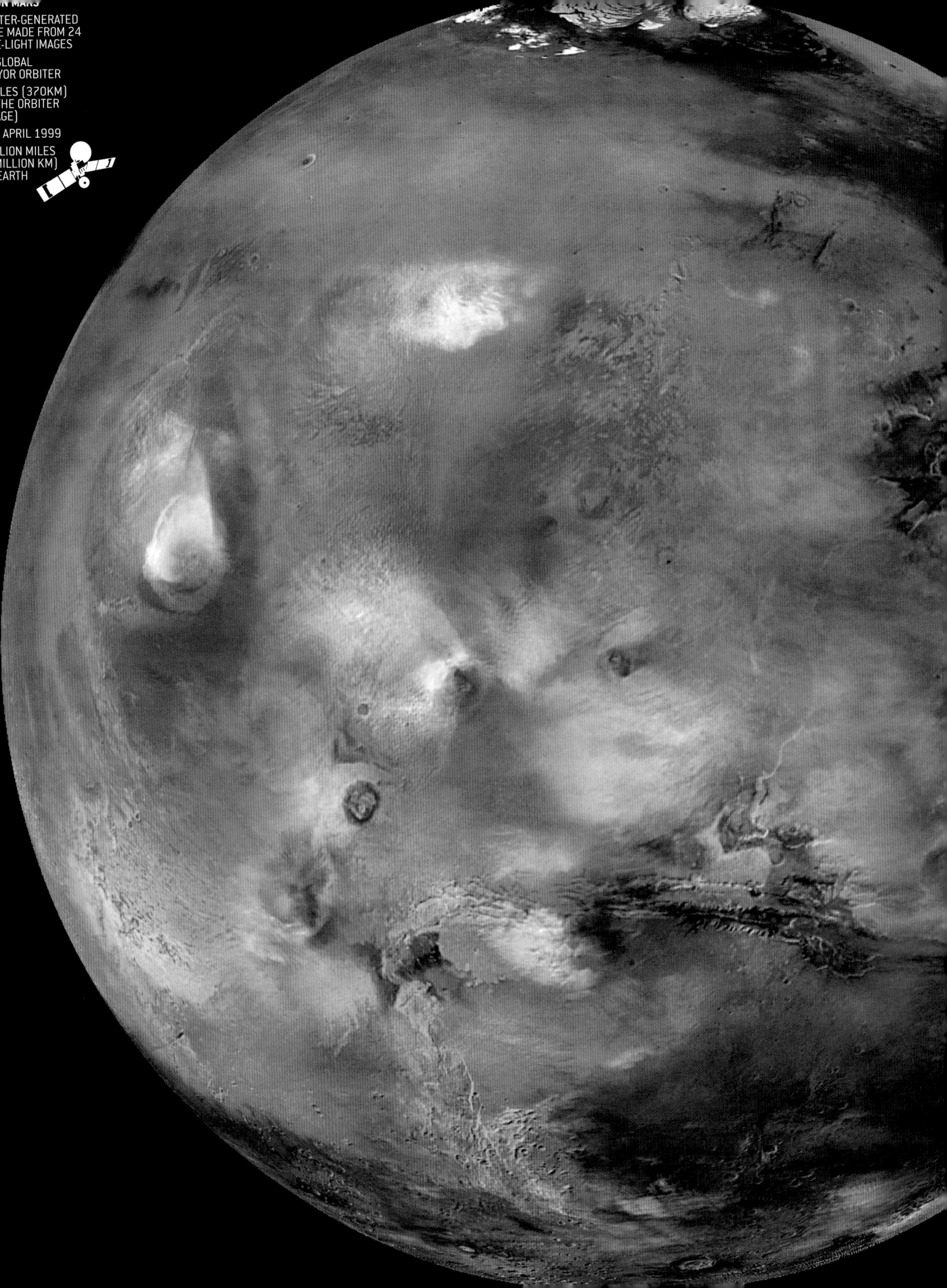

MARS

With its red hue and proximity to Earth, Mars has fascinated man across the centuries. It is the fourth planet in our solar system and the last of the rocky planets orbiting close to the Sun. The Babylonians associated the planet with war and bloodshed. So did other civilizations – the Romans named Mars for their god of war.

The astronomer Giovanni Schiaparelli observed strange markings on the planet in 1877. He called them "canali," which means channels in Italian but was translated incorrectly as "canals." This sparked the Victorian misconception that Mars was populated by an alien race of innovative canal builders.

The focus of current exploration has been water. Water is so important because it offers the tantalizing possibility of life as we understand it. In 2004, the Mars Exploration Rovers (MERs) Spirit and Opportunity found proof of past liquid water in various surface features. The bedrock of Gusev Crater indicates an ancient body of salt water. Evidence of a body of water larger than the Baltic Sea exists in the Terra Meridiani region. "Every single rock has shown signs of alteration by liquid water," said lead investigator Dr Steven Squyres.

Three-dimensional images released from the Mars Express spacecraft in early 2005 show evidence of past gigantic waterfalls, huge glaciers and grand outflow channels. Near the equator, along the Elysium Plains, one photograph shows what appears to be a

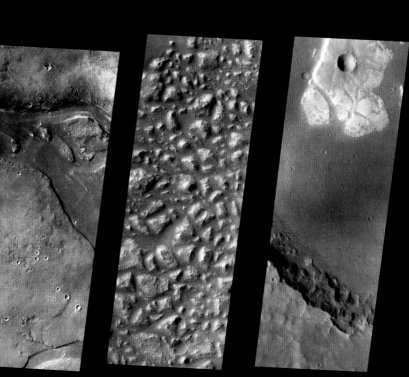

A CHANNEL IN TINJAR VALLIS (VALLEY) CARVED BY WATER OR VOLCANIC LAVA (LEFT)
20 OCTOBER 2002
235 MILLION MILES (378 MILLION KM) FROM EARTH

KNOBS AND MESAS IN ATLANTIS CHAOS REGION PROBABLY FORMED BY EROSION (CENTER)
30 MAY 2002
232 MILLION MILES (373 MILLION KM) FROM EARTH

A CRATER IN THE POLAR REGION SURROUNDED BY SEDIMENTARY ROCK OR VOLCANIC ASH (RIGHT)
18 NOVEMBER 2003
55 MILLION MILES (89 MILLION KM) FROM EARTH

ALL 3 IMAGES: VISIBLE-LIGHT IMAGES (COLOR ENHANCED)
2001 MARS ODYSSEY (MARS-ORBITING)
249 MILES (400KM) FROM ODYSSEY TO MARS (MEAN ALTITUDE)

five-million-year-old frozen sea of water that has been protected from vaporizing by a layer of volcanic ash. Comparable in size and depth to the North Sea, the area features large irregular plates similar in pattern to the pack ice at Earth's poles.

Following the water trail away from the sea leads to a series of fissures known as the Cerberus Fossae. These fractures in the surface were the source of both lava and water floods millions of years ago. In fact, lava plains from the floods are located in eastern Elysium.

The find is captivating because on Earth microorganisms have been found around deep-sea thermal vents. If the Elysium sea water was warmed by past geothermal energy, perhaps it provided the environment for life to develop in a similar form on Mars.

The recent detection of small amounts of methane in the Martian atmosphere is further intriguing evidence for living microorganisms on the planet. Methane is a common byproduct of life on Earth, but it can also be produced by non-biological processes. Volcanoes could be one source, but there is no proof of active volcanism on Mars today. Still, all other possible causes must be ruled out before concluding that methane is a biotracer of present-day life on the planet.

The atmosphere on Mars is thin, composed mainly of carbon dioxide gas. There are clouds, mist and fog, but the

atmosphere lacks the insulation to prevent wide temperature swings, as much as 180°F (100°C) from day to night.

Because of the tenuous atmosphere, water on Mars behaves like carbon dioxide on Earth: Frozen water doesn't melt, it goes directly from ice to vapor without an intervening liquid state. This process, known as sublimation, poses a dilemma for scientists in explaining what appears to be

considerable erosion on the surface. If water flowed, it must have been at a time when the atmosphere was much denser.

The weather report for Mars is cold. Surface temperatures average −65°F (−53°C) and even during the summer rarely rise above the freezing point of water (32°F/0°C). Variations in temperature across the surface produce strong winds, often stirring massive summer dust storms that engulf the

MARS: THE SEARCH FOR WATER

planet. Summers are warmer and shorter in the southern hemisphere than in the north, and the seasons are influenced by the polar ice caps. The main reservoir of water on the planet is concentrated in ice at the north and south poles, although enormous quantities of water ice may exist underground at low latitudes.

The Martian hemispheres are a mismatched pair. The southern terrain is more ancient and heavily cratered, with obvious valley networks possibly formed by past rivers. Along the equator is Valles Marineris. Grander than the Grand Canyon, it is a system of deep canyons that spans an extraordinary 2,500 miles (4,000km). The younger northern plains show indications of former lake beds, and volcanoes dot the landscape. The north's most imposing feature, Olympus Mons, is the largest volcano in our solar system – a hundred times larger than Mauna Loa, the largest on Earth.

Mars's changing seasons, ice caps, clouds, volcanoes and canyons make for similarities with Earth. But that is where the similarity ends. Mars is rocky, cold and barren. It has two moons, Phobos (meaning fear) and Deimos (meaning panic). The entire Martian planet is about the size of Earth's iron core. The planet's red color is derived from the presence of olivine and iron oxide on its surface. It is as if the whole planet is coated in rust.

M

ENDURANCE CRATER IN MERIDIANI PLANUM REGION (TOP)
APPROXIMATE TRUE-COLOR MOSAIC PANORAMA MADE OVER SEVEN SOLS (MARTIAN DAYS)
VISIBLE-LIGHT IMAGE
MARS EXPLORATION ROVER OPPORTUNITY
CRATER DIAMETER IS 427 FEET (130M)
23–29 MAY 2004
218 MILLION MILES (350 MILLION KM) FROM EARTH

SELF-PORTRAIT OF OPPORTUNITY IN SHADOW INSIDE ENDURANCE CRATER (OPPOSITE)
VISIBLE-LIGHT IMAGE
26 JULY 2004
31.5 FEET (9.6M) FROM OPPORTUNITY TO TIP OF SHADOW
243 MILLION MILES (391 MILLION KM) FROM EARTH

MICROSCOPIC VIEW INSIDE EAGLE CRATER IN MERIDIANI PLANUM REGION (ABOVE)
IRON-RICH PEBBLES SHOW EVIDENCE OF PAST WATER
VISIBLE-LIGHT IMAGE
4 INCHES (100MM) FROM OPPORTUNITY
16 FEBRUARY 2004
143 MILLION MILES (230 MILLION KM) FROM EARTH

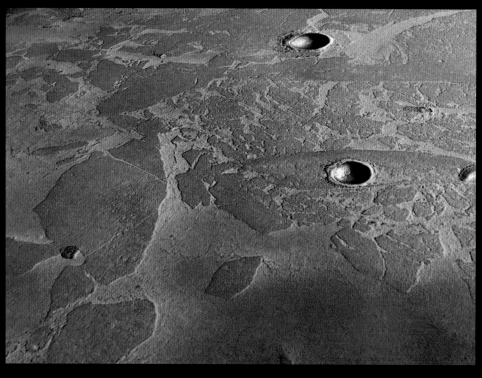

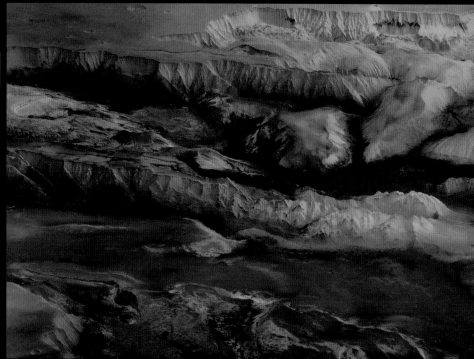

MARS SCAPES

A FROZEN SEA NEAR THE EQUATOR IS THOUGHT TO BE PROTECTED FROM VAPORIZING BY A COATING OF VOLCANIC ASH (TOP)

THE TWO IMPACT CRATERS WERE FORMED BEFORE THE AREA WAS FLOODED. RUBBLE PILES AROUND THE CRATERS PROVIDED CLUES TO A FROZEN SEA.

VISIBLE-LIGHT IMAGE (NEAR TRUE COLOR)

MARS EXPRESS

162 MILES (260KM) FROM MARS EXPRESS

19 JANUARY 2004

118,380 MILLION MILES (190,505 MILLION KM) FROM EARTH

THE CENTRAL AREA OF VALLES MARINERIS CANYON, WHICH IS LARGER THAN THE GRAND CANYON IN THE U.S. (ABOVE)

SULFATE MINERALS FOUND IN LAYERS OF SEDIMENT INDICATE PAST WATER ACTIVITY IN THE CANYON

VISIBLE-LIGHT MOSAIC (NEAR TRUE COLOR)

MARS EXPRESS

24 APRIL 2004, 2 MAY 2004

326 MILES (525KM), 466 MILES (750KM) FROM MARS EXPRESS

200 MILLION MILES (325 MILLION KM) FROM EARTH

KASEI VALLIS, ONE OF THE LARGEST CHANNELS ON MARS, CARVED BY GLACIERS OR WATER-RELATED OUTFLOWS (RIGHT)

VISIBLE-LIGHT IMAGE (NEAR TRUE COLOR)

MARS EXPRESS

169 MILES (272KM) FROM MARS EXPRESS

29 JANUARY 2004

127 MILLION MILES (204 MILLION KM) FROM EARTH

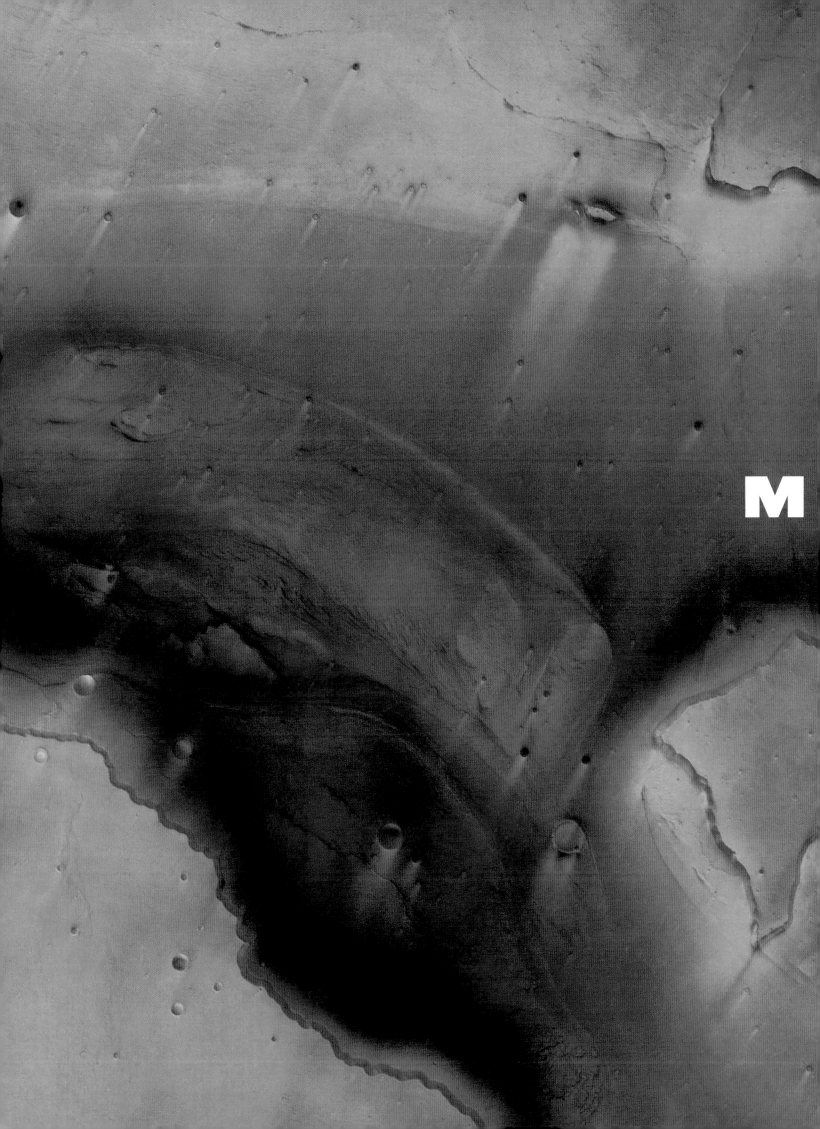

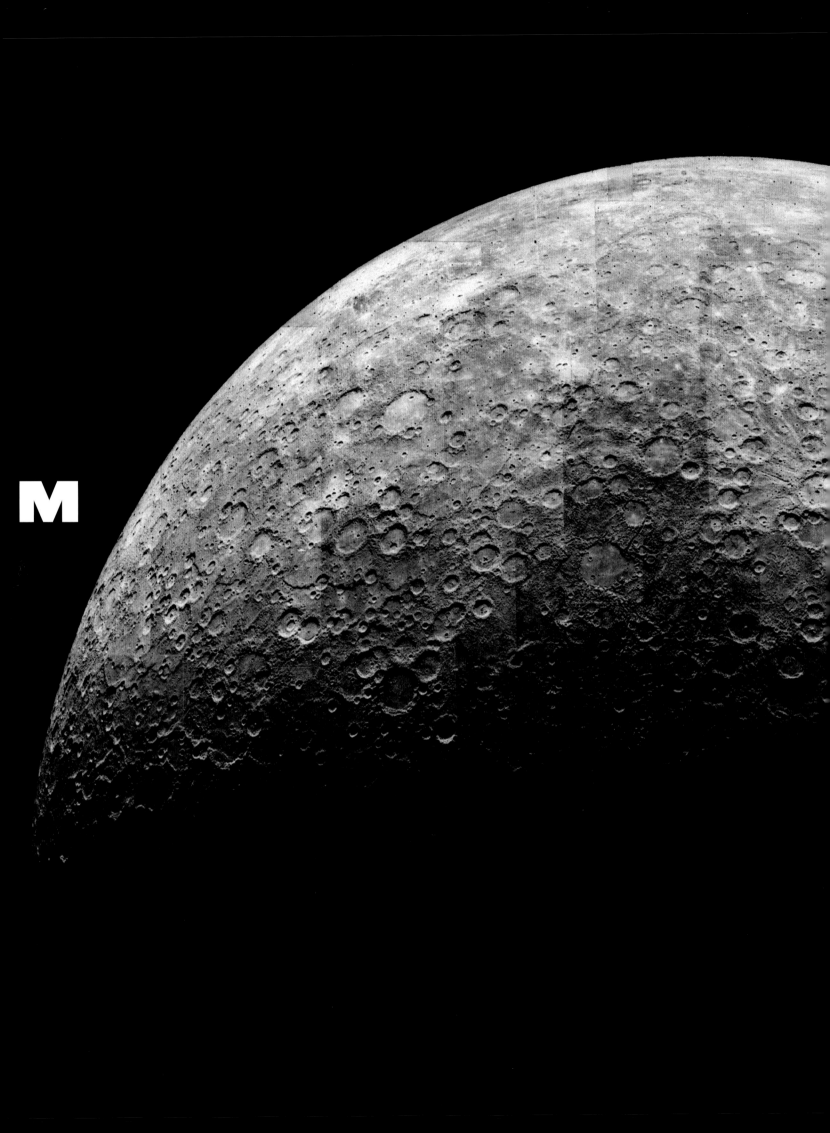

MERCURY

MERCURY IS THE PLANET CLOSEST to the Sun and the fastest in the solar system. Named for Mercurius, the Roman god of speed, commerce and travel, Mercury races through space at 31 miles (50km) a second, circling the Sun in just 88 Earth days. Its elliptical orbit carries it as close as 29 million miles (47 million km) to the Sun and as far away as 44 million miles (71 million km). In contrast to its speedy orbit around the Sun, Mercury's rotation on its axis is extremely slow: 59 Earth days. In fact, it is so slow that a full day on Mercury – sunrise to sunrise – takes 176 Earth days.

Mercury's temperature fluctuations are also the most extreme in the solar system, a result of both the planet's proximity to the Sun and the absence of a protective atmosphere. Temperatures on the "day" or Sun side of the planet can soar as high as 873°F (467°C); on the "night" side, they can plummet to −303°F (−186°C). With no atmosphere to protect its surface, Mercury also has no defense against meteorites; like Earth's Moon, much of its surface is scarred by impact craters from collisions with meteors.

Mercury has no moons of its own, and until recently was thought to have no water. In 1991, astronomers studying the planet using radar reported that Mercury may have water ice at its north pole. The evidence exists deep inside craters where the Sun does not shine.

MERCURY
MOSAIC OF VISIBLE-LIGHT IMAGES
MARINER 10 SPACECRAFT
125,000 MILES
(201,000KM) FROM MARINER 10
MARCH 1974–MARCH 1975
48–138 MILLION MILES
(77–222 MILLION KM)
FROM EARTH

THE MICE

"THE MICE" IS A NICKNAME FOR A pair of colliding galaxies, NGC 4676 A and B, located 300 million light-years away in the constellation Coma Berenices.

Galaxies can interact over the course of millions and millions of years. Gravitational forces sometimes pull galaxies toward each other. The interac-

M

tion may result in a merger and distortion. The Mice are galaxies "caught in the act" of merging. They are typical of tadpole objects seen throughout the universe. These objects have a tail and one or two bright heads, which indicates that two galaxies are in the process of colliding.

The long straight tails consist of clusters of young stars formed from the gravitational collapse of gas and dust. Computer simulations suggest that the Mice are two nearly identical spiral galaxies that encountered each other approximately 160 million years ago. When they do finally merge, they will form an elliptical galaxy.

THE MICE (NGC 4676 A AND B) IN THE CONSTELLATION COMA BERENICES

THESE NEARLY IDENTICAL COLLIDING SPIRAL GALAXIES EVENTUALLY WILL MERGE INTO AN ELLIPTICAL GALAXY

VISIBLE-LIGHT IMAGE

HUBBLE SPACE TELESCOPE (EARTH ORBITING)

7 APRIL 2002

ABOUT 300 MILLION LIGHT-YEARS FROM EARTH

M

MOLECULAR CLOUD

CLOSE-UP OF THE "PILLARS OF CREATION" (LEFT) **EMERGING FROM A WALL OF MOLECULAR HYDROGEN IN THE EAGLE NEBULA** (RIGHT)

INSIDE THESE DENSE GASEOUS PILLARS KNOWN AS ELEPHANT TRUNKS, YOUNG STARS ARE FORMING

VISIBLE-LIGHT IMAGE

HUBBLE SPACE TELESCOPE (EARTH-ORBITING)

1 APRIL 1995

6,500 LIGHT-YEARS FROM EARTH

M Visible sites of star birth in our galaxy, the emission nebulas are strung along the glowing stellar lane of our Milky Way as seen from Earth. These nebulas resemble campfires in a forest viewed from far away. What can't be observed in visible light is the underlying "forest" that is made up of giant molecular clouds that store most of the star-forming mass of our galaxy.

Molecular clouds lie along the spiral arms of a galaxy where dust and gas pile up and compress along a density wave. They are so cold that primeval hydrogen atoms bond together in pairs. Hidden from the destructive blowtorch of radiation from stars, some areas embedded deep within a cloud are so cold they are near absolute zero (−460°F/−273°C). Most of the hydrogen gas buried inside a molecular cloud is laced with trace elements such as oxygen and nitrogen, and with fine dust grains of carbon and silicon that are even smaller than smoke particles.

Giant molecular clouds can be hundreds of light-years across. They are 100,000 times denser than the atoms found in normal space between stars. Still, there are about one quadrillion more atoms inside a ping-pong ball than in an equivalent piece of a molecular cloud. Dark molecular clouds are turbulent, clumpy and chaotic. Light-year-wide globules buried deep inside these clouds fragment and condense, precipitating a flurry of star formation. About 10,000 solar-type stars are born inside each giant molecular cloud.

The torrential energy of new-born stars eats out gaseous caverns inside these clouds, like holes in Swiss cheese. Some burst out as brightly glowing "blisters" on the edges of molecular clouds. One of the best known of the glowing "blisters" is the Eagle Nebula.

WIDE-VIEW IMAGE OF THE EAGLE NEBULA (M 16) (RIGHT)

RADIATION FROM NEWBORN STARS HAS CARVED OUT THIS AREA OF A GIANT MOLECULAR CLOUD

VISIBLE-LIGHT IMAGE THROUGH 3 FILTERS (REPRESENTATIVE COLOR)

NSF 0.9M TELESCOPE AT KITT PEAK NATIONAL OBSERVATORY, NOAO

15 JUNE 2000

6,500 LIGHT-YEARS FROM EARTH

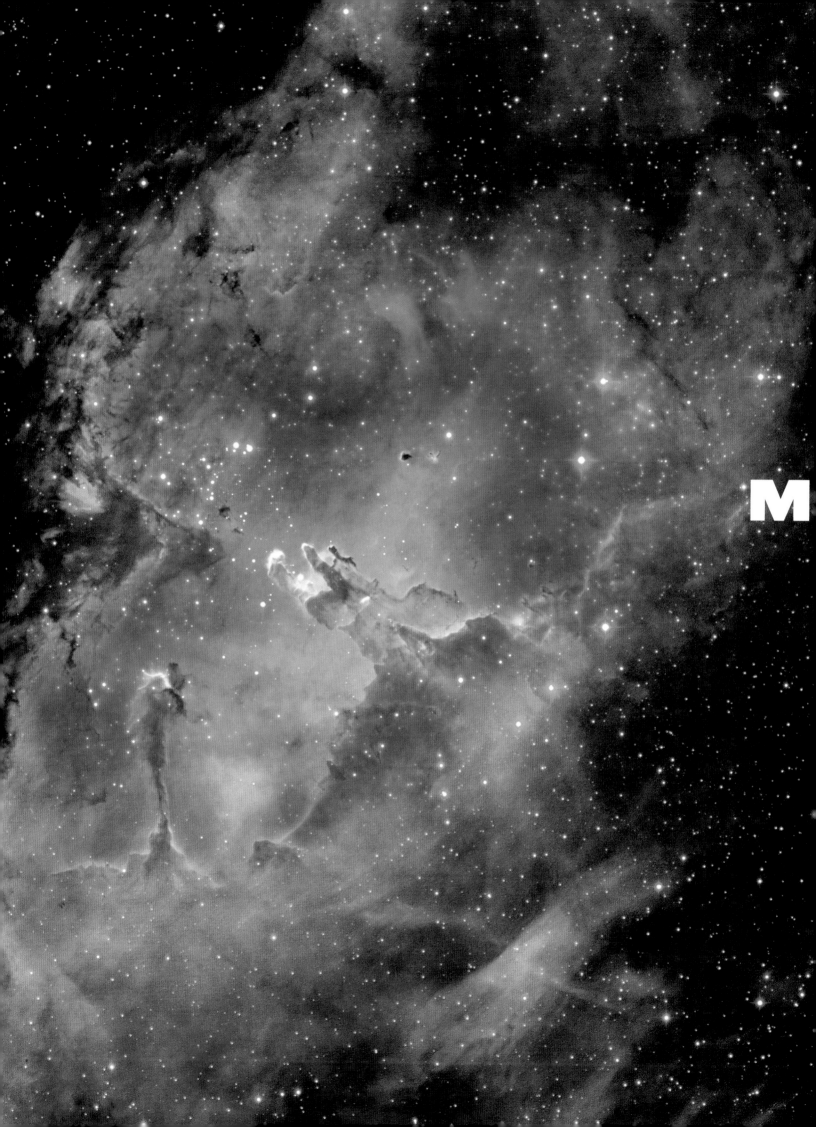

M

EARTH'S SATELLITE MOON
(LEFT)

DARK LAVA-FILLED MARIA
IN NORTHERN HEMISPHERE

NORTH POLAR MOSAIC OF
18 VISIBLE-LIGHT IMAGES

GALILEO ORBITER

564,000 MILES (908,000KM)
FROM GALILEO

7 DECEMBER 1992

241,000 MILES
(389,000KM)
FROM EARTH

EARTHRISE OBSERVED
FROM LUNAR ORBIT
(RIGHT)

VISIBLE-LIGHT IMAGE

HANDHELD 70MM
HASSELBLAD THROUGH
MODULE WINDOW

APOLLO 17

DECEMBER 1972

239,000 MILES
(384,000KM)
APOLLO TO EARTH

MOON

"MAGNIFICENT DESOLATENESS" IS how men who have walked on the Moon have described it. And although it is the only extraterrestrial body on which humans have landed, there is still so much we do not understand. It is a barren, cratered sphere, with no water or atmosphere, that orbits the Earth. Sometimes visible and sometimes vanished, it is always mysterious. The Moon is like a place that you cannot completely know, a place that always keeps some secrets.

Myth and mystery have surrounded our understanding of the Moon from ancient times. According to superstition, a full Moon causes madness. The word lunatic comes from "luna," the Latin word for moon, and it literally means moonstruck. Europeans thought they saw the face of the "man in the moon," while Mayans believed they saw the face of a rabbit. Through the ages, the Moon has been a favorite subject for writers. In the 19th century, Jules Verne helped popularize science fiction when he wrote about space travel in stories such as FROM THE EARTH TO THE MOON.

Some of the allure may be due to the Moon's changing faces, or phases. The Moon orbits Earth about once every month, and as it does, its apparent shape changes from a round ball, called a full Moon, to nothing at all, known as a new Moon.

Because the Moon does not produce its own light, we see only the half that is lit by the Sun. And we always see the same side of the Moon, the near side, because it is in

M

synchronous rotation with the Earth. This means that it takes the same amount of time for the Moon to rotate on its own axis as it does to revolve around the Earth, 27.3 days.

Scientists are not sure how the Moon was formed. Many believe that it was created when an asteroid or small planetary body collided with Earth four-and-a-half billion years ago. That collision threw debris into orbit, which eventually joined together to become the Moon.

The Moon was hot and molten in the beginning. Over time, it cooled and formed a cratered outer layer, or mantle, and an iron core. There are two basic types of terrain on the Moon's near side: light, cratered highlands called terrae (Latin for lands) surround darker, smoother maria (meaning seas, because they were once thought to be bodies of water). The craters were probably caused by the impact of meteorites on the Moon's surface; the largest are known as walled plains.

The moon has no atmosphere, and its gravity is weak — about one-sixth of Earth's. This means that a person who weighs 180 pounds (82kg) on Earth would weigh only 30 pounds (14kg) on the Moon. This proved to be a big help to the astronauts who went to the Moon because their spacesuits, equipped with life-support systems, were very heavy. On 20 July 1969 — only 66 years after the Wright Brothers first flew — the American spacecraft APOLLO 11 landed on the Sea of Tranquillity, and Neil Armstrong became the first person to set foot on the Moon.

M

THE MARE ORIENTALE IMPACT BASIN STRADDLES THE NEAR AND FAR SIDES OF THE MOON
VISIBLE-LIGHT MOSAIC
LUNAR ORBITER 4
1,700 MILES (2,700KM) FROM ORBITER
25 MAY 1967
239,000 MILES (384,000KM) FROM EARTH

MOON: ORIENTAL BASIN

THE ORIENTAL BASIN, OR MARE Orientale, is viewed from Earth on the eastern rim of the Moon, at the boundary of its near and far sides. It is observable face on only from a spacecraft.

The saucer-shaped depression, formed more than three billion years ago by an asteroid, measures 600 miles (1,000km) across. It consists of a shallow basin surrounded by three concentric rings of mountains, giving it the appearance of a bull's-eye. Like some 40 other craters on the Moon, this spectacular impact basin is called a mare, the Latin word for sea, because early astronomers believed these huge dark areas might be oceans. There is, of course, no water on the Moon.

Maria cover about 30 percent of the Moon's surface. Most are dark, flat regions that show evidence of past volcanic lava flow. Mare Orientale, the youngest of the Moon's impact basins, is not dark because it never filled with lava. Its basalt crust is also much shallower than those of Earth-facing mare, probably less than a mile deep.

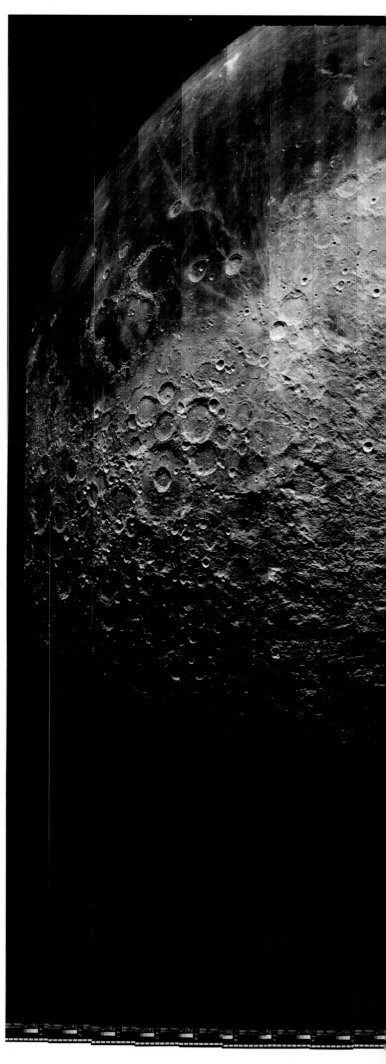

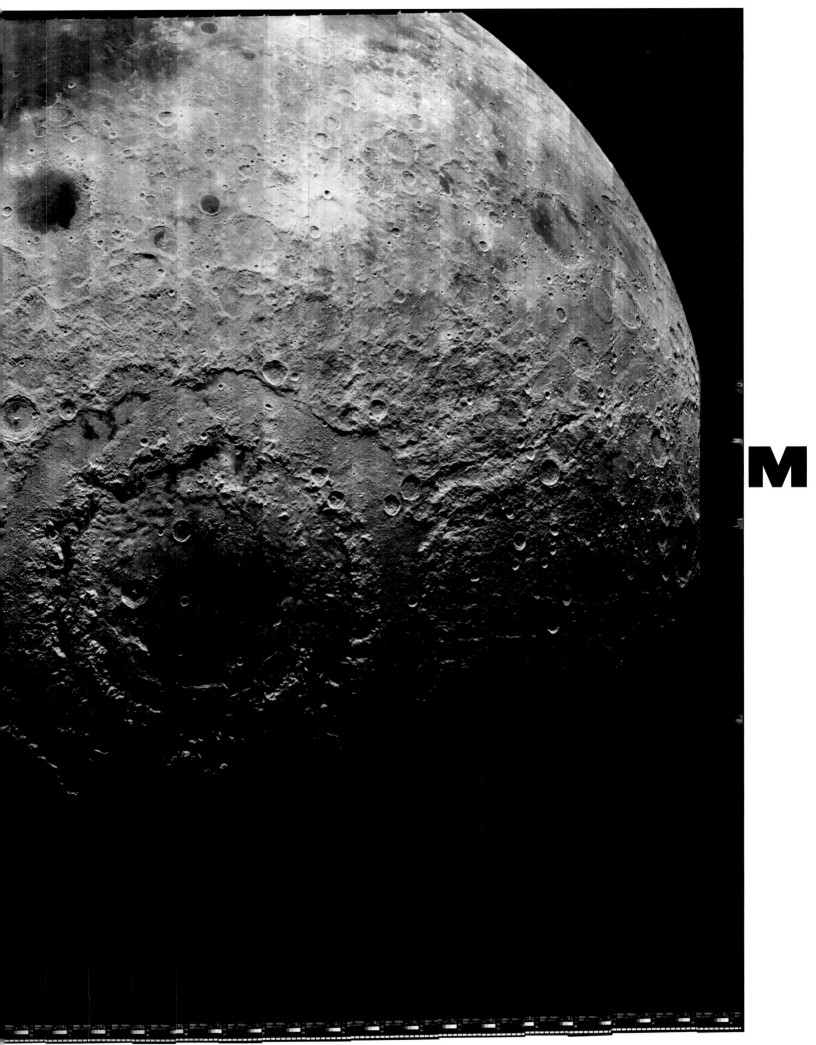

M

APOLLO 17: THE LAST MISSION

"ABSOLUTELY INCREDIBLE — YOU can see the boulder tracks — there are boulders all over," said Harrison Schmitt, the only geologist ever to explore the Moon.

The flight of APOLLO 17 marked the end of an era. It was the last mission to land men on the Moon in the 20th century, and it is considered by many to be the capstone of NASA's Project Apollo.

In December 1972, the crew landed in the Taurus-Littrow region, a valley on the rim of the Sea of Serenity, and sur-veyed the geology of the land-scape. The landing site was selected because it offered young volcanic rock as well as older mountainous wall materi-al. The astronauts returned with the richest collection of rock and soil samples of any Apollo mission, 243 pounds (110kg).

APOLLO 17 is memorable for other reasons. The astronauts remained on the lunar surface for 75 hours and covered more dis-tance in the Lunar Rover Vehicle (or LRV, a four-wheeled manually controlled electric cart) than any

M

Geologist Schmitt uses a custom-made stainless steel rake to collect rock and soil samples. (122.26.17 HOURS INTO MISSION)

An ancient boulder, thrown here by the impact that created the Sea of Serenity,

other astronauts — 22 miles (35km). They also took 2,218 photographs, many of them shot sequentially for panoramic views. Schmitt and Mission Commander Eugene Cernan hold the distinction of being the last humans to walk on the lunar surface.

EUGENE CERNAN AND HARRISON SCHMITT EXPLORE THE TAURUS-LITTROW VALLEY, SEA OF SERENITY

VISIBLE-LIGHT IMAGES
70MM HASSELBLADS ATTACHED TO THE ASTRONAUTS' PRESSURE SUITS AT CHEST HEIGHT
APOLLO 17
DECEMBER 1972
239,000 MILES (384,000KM) FROM EARTH

Schmitt (shadow at left) photographs Cernan removing tools from the LRV. At far left is the Apollo Lunar Surface Experiments Package. (120.48.56 HOURS INTO MISSION)

M

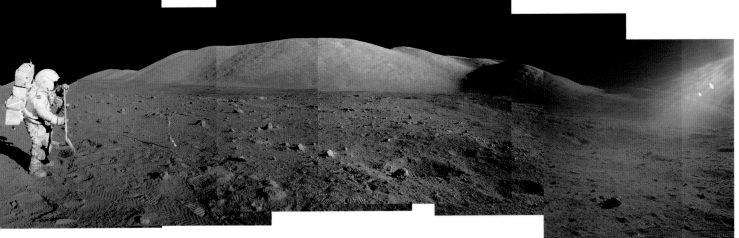

is named Tracy's Rock, for Cernan's daughter. (165.00.58 HOURS INTO MISSION)

NEBULA

SPACE IS NOT EMPTY. IT IS FILLED with what we call "interstellar matter." This is a mix of gases — mostly hydrogen and helium — and dust, made up of elements such as carbon and silicon. This interstellar matter is the raw material of stars and galaxies. Interstellar matter can clump together to form clouds of gas and dust known as nebulas (from the Latin for cloud). A single nebula may contain enough matter to produce tens of thousands of stars.

We classify nebulas by how they appear to us. The dense and compact clouds of dark nebulas, for example, are not clearly visible in the night sky. But we can make them out when they block the light from stars or glowing gases behind them. Other nebulas are brightly lit. Reflection nebulas reflect the light cast by stars. Emission nebulas are lit from within by the radiation of gas molecules excited by stars inside the nebulas.

Nebulas are key players in the birth of stars. The process begins with the contraction of dark globules within the nebula. Globules contract until they collapse under the force of their own gravity, precipitating the birth of stars.

Although emission nebulas are associated with star birth, other glowing nebulas are on hand when stars die. These are known as planetary nebulas. They are formed by the gas and dust released by some dying stars — stars the size of our Sun. This means we can expect to see a planetary nebula in about five billion years, when the life span of our Sun comes to an end.

ORION NEBULA COMPLEX

ORION IS ONE OF THE BEST-known constellations. It is large in the sky and easy to see. The red supergiant star Betelgeuse sits at the mythical warrior's right shoulder, the brilliant blue supergiant Rigel at his left foot, and three clearly defined stars, almost as bright, form his belt.

Clouds of gas and dust envelop the constellation, which is home to a rich array of nebulas, known as the Orion Nebula Complex. Producing tens of thousands of stars within the past ten million years, the complex is typical of regions throughout the galaxy that are prolific in stellar birth.

Close to Orion's belt is the most famous of all nebulas, the Horsehead Nebula (left, to the right of center). A dark nebula, the Horsehead rears up out of the gloom, silhouetted against the red glow of a large emission nebula. To the left of the Horsehead is Alnitak, the most southerly star in Orion's belt. Below Alnitak is the Flame Nebula, an emission nebula whose hidden stars cast a curious yellow glow.

Set in the hilt of Orion's sword is the Great Nebula of Orion itself (next page). Bright enough to be seen by the naked eye, it is an emission nebula lit by several huge, hot stars at its center. These are the Trapezium stars (the four brightest form a trapezoid). Near the nebula's core are also approximately one thousand young stars.

A COMMUNITY OF NEBULAS IN ORION'S BELT
VISIBLE-LIGHT COMPOSITE
ANGLO-AUSTRALIAN OBSERVATORY/
ROYAL OBSERVATORY EDINBURGH
OCTOBER 1979
1,400 LIGHT-YEARS FROM EARTH

N

**GREAT NEBULA
OF ORION (M 42)**
(ABOVE)

AN EMISSION NEBULA
ILLUMINATED BY HOT
STARS AT ITS CORE

VISIBLE-LIGHT IMAGE

CANADA-FRANCE-
HAWAII TELESCOPE

2003

1,500 LIGHT-YEARS
FROM EARTH

CONSTELLATION ORION
(LEFT)

STARS IN THE CONSTELLATION
ARE AWASH IN NEBULAS

VISIBLE-LIGHT IMAGE
BY BILL AND SALLY FLETCHER

PENTAX 6X7CM CAMERA
WITH 90MM LENS

24 OCTOBER 1998

1,600 LIGHT-YEARS
FROM EARTH

**HORSEHEAD NEBULA
(BARNARD 33)**

A GIGANTIC
DARK NEBULA
OBSCURES LIGHT
FROM EMISSION
NEBULA IC 434

VISIBLE-LIGHT IMAGE

CANADA-FRANCE-
HAWAII TELESCOPE

2001

1,500 LIGHT-YEARS
FROM EARTH

NEPTUNE

N

Named after the Roman god of the sea, Neptune is the most distant gas giant in our solar system, and the eighth planet from the Sun, a vast 2.8 billion miles (4.5 billion km) away. However, because of Pluto's elliptical orbit, Neptune is actually the farthest planet from the Sun for a 20-year period every 248 Earth years.

Neptune was the first planet discovered as a result of mathematical calculation rather than astronomical observation. Studying irregularities in the motion of Uranus, scientists posited the gravitational pull of a larger, then unknown, planet.

Because of Neptune's distance from the Sun, its orbit takes 165 years. That means the planet has not yet completed a full circle since its discovery in 1846. The distance also makes it impossible to see with the naked eye.

Neptune and Uranus are essentially twins in size. Neptune is slightly smaller in diameter but slightly larger in mass. Neptune's interior is also similar to its twin – composed of the melted ices of water, methane and ammonia with a rocky core about the size of Earth. Hydrogen, helium and methane gas make up its atmosphere. The methane absorbs red from the illuminating sunlight, giving Neptune its blue color. And the planet's winds are strong, the fastest in the solar system.

Neptune has a ring system and 13 known moons. Triton is not only the largest of Neptune's moons, it is also the largest moon in the solar system with a retrograde orbit.

N

NEPTUNE WITH ITS GREAT DARK SPOT, A HURRICANELIKE STORM (TOP LEFT)

VISIBLE-LIGHT IMAGE

VOYAGER 2

4.4 MILLION MILES (7 MILLION KM) FROM VOYAGER 2

21 AUGUST 1989

3 BILLION MILES (4.8 BILLION KM) FROM EARTH

NEPTUNE'S SOUTH POLE (MAIN IMAGE)

VISIBLE-LIGHT IMAGE

VOYAGER 2

20 AUGUST 1989

MARS'S SATELLITE PHOBOS
VISIBLE-LIGHT COMPOSITE
VIKING 1 ORBITER
988 MILES (1,590KM)
FROM VIKING
10 JUNE 1977
5,900 MILES (9,500KM)
FROM PHOBOS TO MARS

PHOBOS

THE MOON PHOBOS WAS NAMED for a son of Mars, the Roman god of war. Phobos is the larger of Mars's two moons; the other is Deimos. Phobos measures 17 by 12 miles (28 by 20 km), and it circles the planet three times a Martian day.

The moon's most distinctive feature is Stickney, a six-mile-wide (10km) crater that was first identified in pictures from the Mariner 9 mission and later from the Viking 1 orbiter. Stickney was named after Chloe Angeline Stickney Hall, the wife of Asaph Hall, the astronomer who discovered both Phobos and Deimos. The massive impact that formed the crater nearly destroyed Phobos and created streak patterns across the surface.

Phobos has no atmosphere, and its surface seems to consist of powder created by the constant bombardment of meteorites. The moon is composed of a carbon-rich rock similar to that found in certain asteroids.

The atmosphereless Phobos rapidly loses heat after sunset. As a result, the moon exhibits extremes in temperature from its day and night sides. Temperatures range from a high of about 25°F (−4°C) to a low of −170°F (−112°C).

The satellite's end is predictable. It will crash into Mars or break up in a ring. Approaching Mars at a rate of six feet (1.8m) every hundred years, Phobos is expected to collide with its planet in approximately 50 million years.

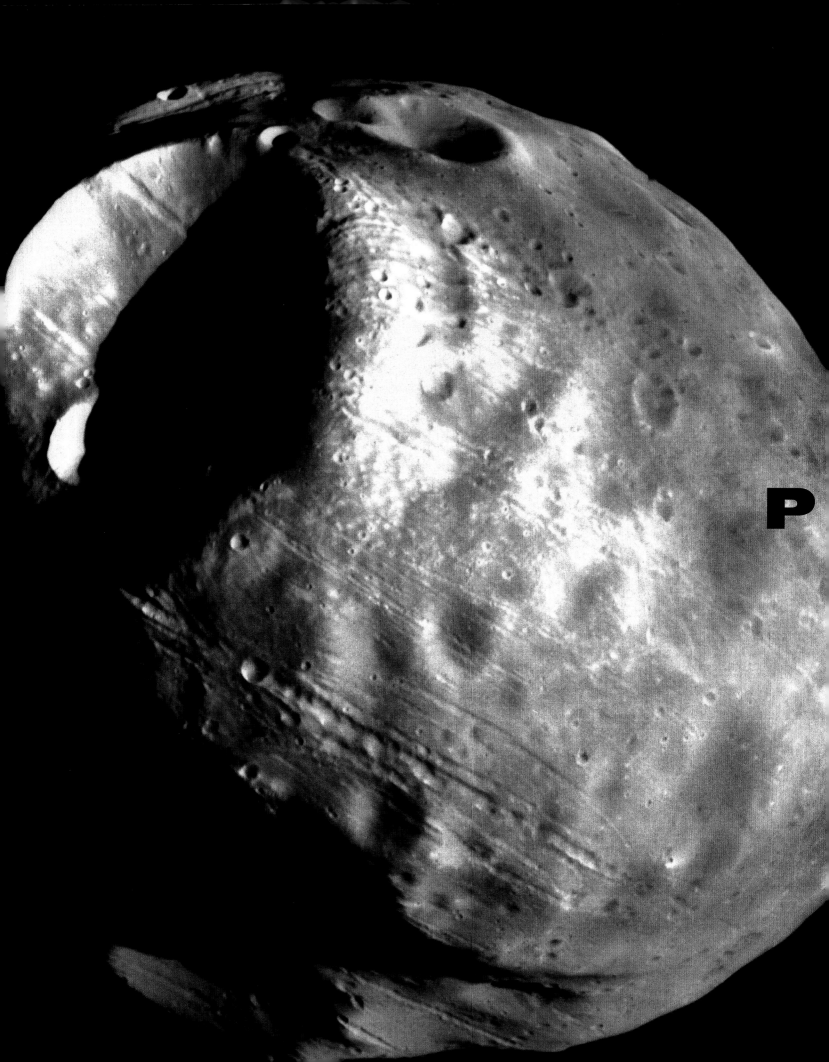

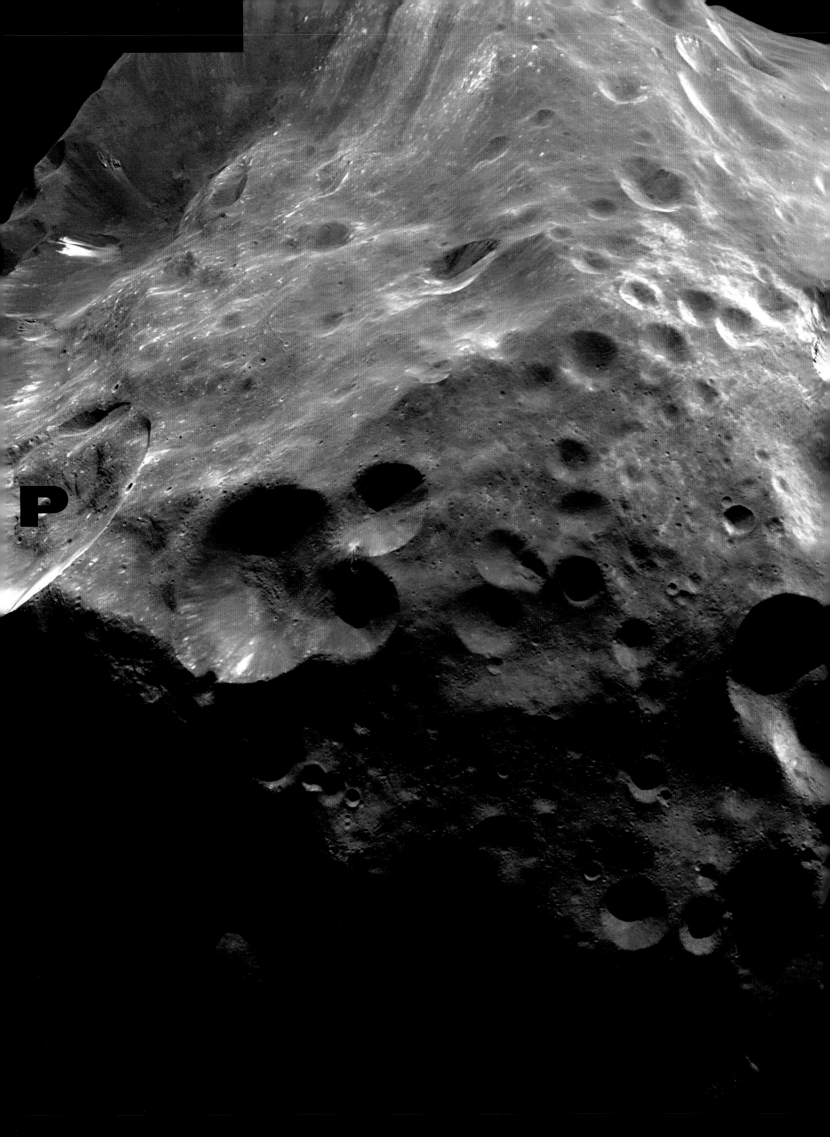

P

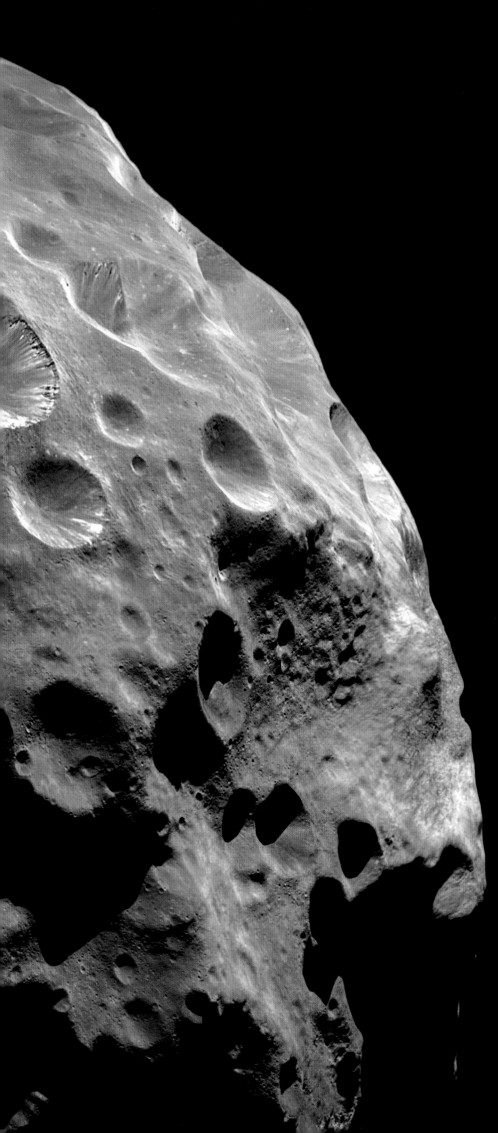

PHOEBE

According to data sent back from the Cassini spacecraft, Saturn's moon Phoebe is probably a frozen remnant from the formation of the solar system more than four billion years ago. Readings from Cassini confirm that Phoebe is composed of a primordial mixture of ice, rock and carbon. Surprisingly, Phoebe's composition seems to be more like a comet than a typical rocky moon.

What distinguishes Phoebe is its orbit. About 132 miles (212km) wide, the satellite turns on its axis every nine hours and takes roughly 18 months to complete a revolution around Saturn. But it orbits Saturn in retrograde, the opposite direction of most other moons and objects in the solar system. It also orbits far away from Saturn – eight million miles (13 million km).

Unlike most Saturnian moons, Phoebe reflects very little sunlight. Phoebe's darkness and its retrograde orbit have led scientists to speculate that it is a captured object (one that is trapped by the gravity of a bigger body, usually a planet).

Scientists believe that Phoebe and bodies like it were abundant in the outer reaches of the solar system. They formed the building blocks of that part called the Kuiper Belt, a ring-shaped area extending from Neptune outward. Phoebe apparently moved to the inner solar system and then became trapped in Saturn's orbit.

P

SATURN'S SATELLITE PHOEBE
MOSAIC OF 6 VISIBLE-LIGHT IMAGES
CASSINI ORBITER
7,700 MILES (12,400KM)
FROM CASSINI
11 JUNE 2004
8 MILLION MILES
(13 MILLION KM) FROM
PHOEBE TO SATURN

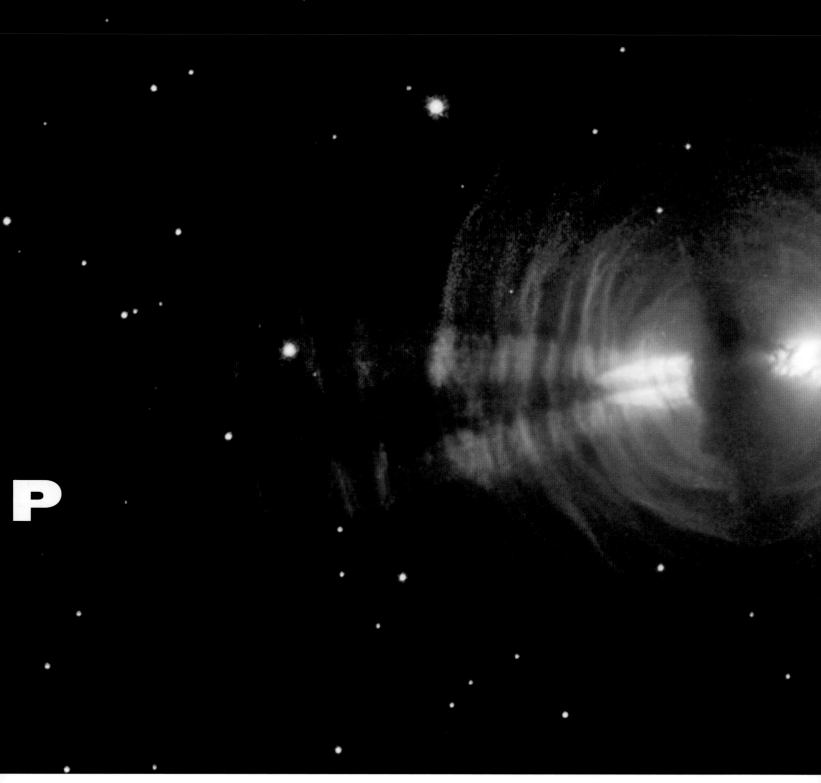

P

PLANETARY NEBULA

role in the death of stars as they do in their birth.

As a star ages and nuclear fusion changes from burning hydrogen to burning helium, the core shrinks and the outer layers expand. The star becomes a red giant, with a diameter that can be as much as a hundred times greater than before. Its gravitational pull weakens, and gas and dust peel away, form-ing a shell of interstellar matter around the exposed core. This gaseous shell is called a planetary nebula, although it has nothing at all to do with planets. It is simply that the astronomer who named them thought that the circular objects he saw resembled planets.

Planetary nebulas glow. In fact, generally they are not con-sidered planetary nebulas until they start to glow. This happens as the dying star's core shrinks on its way to becoming a white dwarf. The gravitational con-traction of the core generates heat, which emits ultraviolet radiation. When this radiation energizes gases in the shell of released matter, the gases fluoresce, emitting radiation of their own in a multicolored glow corresponding to different elements – green (nitrogen), red (hydrogen) and yellow (sulfur).

Planetary nebulas appear in a variety of exotic shapes, such as the multicolored Egg Nebula (above) and the Red Rectangle (right). Some nebulas in the category resemble animals, inviting aptly descriptive nicknames. On the following pages are the Bug Nebula, with its segmented form and winglike shapes, and the Cat's Eye Nebula, with its piercing one-eyed glare.

P

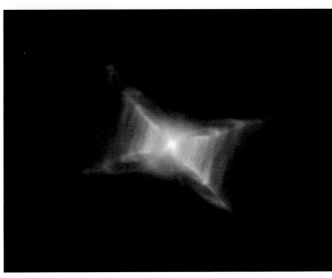

RED RECTANGLE NEBULA (HD 44179) SURROUNDS A DYING STAR (LEFT)

THE LADDERLIKE
STRUCTURES
MAY BE CAUSED
BY MASS EJECTIONS
FROM THE STAR

VISIBLE-LIGHT IMAGE

HUBBLE SPACE TELESCOPE
(EARTH-ORBITING)

17–18 MARCH 1999

2,300 LIGHT-YEARS
FROM EARTH

EGG NEBULA (CRL 2688)
(ABOVE)

POLARIZING FILTERS
REVEAL DUST SHELLS
AND LIGHT BEAMS
RADIATING FROM A
HIDDEN STAR

VISIBLE-LIGHT IMAGE

HUBBLE SPACE TELESCOPE
(EARTH-ORBITING)

SEPTEMBER–OCTOBER 2002

3,000 LIGHT-YEARS
FROM EARTH

P

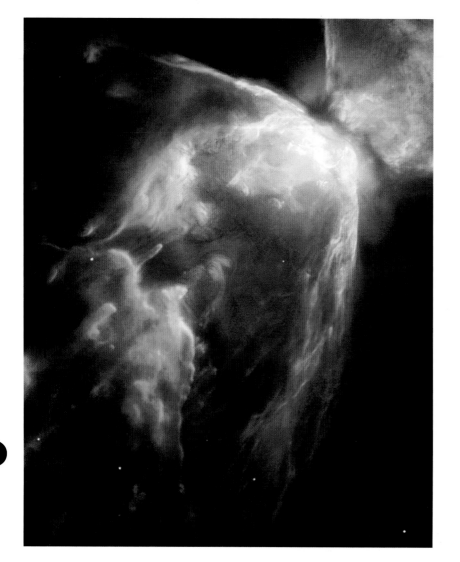

BUG NEBULA (NGC 6302)
(ABOVE)

THIS IS ONE OF THE BRIGHTEST
KNOWN PLANETARY NEBULAS.
THE FIERY, DYING STAR AT
ITS CENTER IS COVERED BY A
BLANKET OF ICY HAILSTONES.

VISIBLE-LIGHT IMAGE

HUBBLE SPACE TELESCOPE
(EARTH-ORBITING)

AUGUST 2000

4,000 LIGHT-YEARS FROM EARTH

CAT'S EYE NEBULA (NGC 6543)
(RIGHT)

THE CONCENTRIC RINGS AROUND THE
CAT'S EYE INDICATE THAT THE DYING
STAR EJECTED ITS MASS IN A SERIES
OF PULSES EVERY 1,500 YEARS.
SUCH RINGS ARE THOUGHT TO BE
COMMON IN PLANETARY NEBULAS.

VISIBLE-LIGHT IMAGE

HUBBLE SPACE TELESCOPE
(EARTH-ORBITING)

4 MAY 2002

3,000 LIGHT-YEARS FROM EARTH

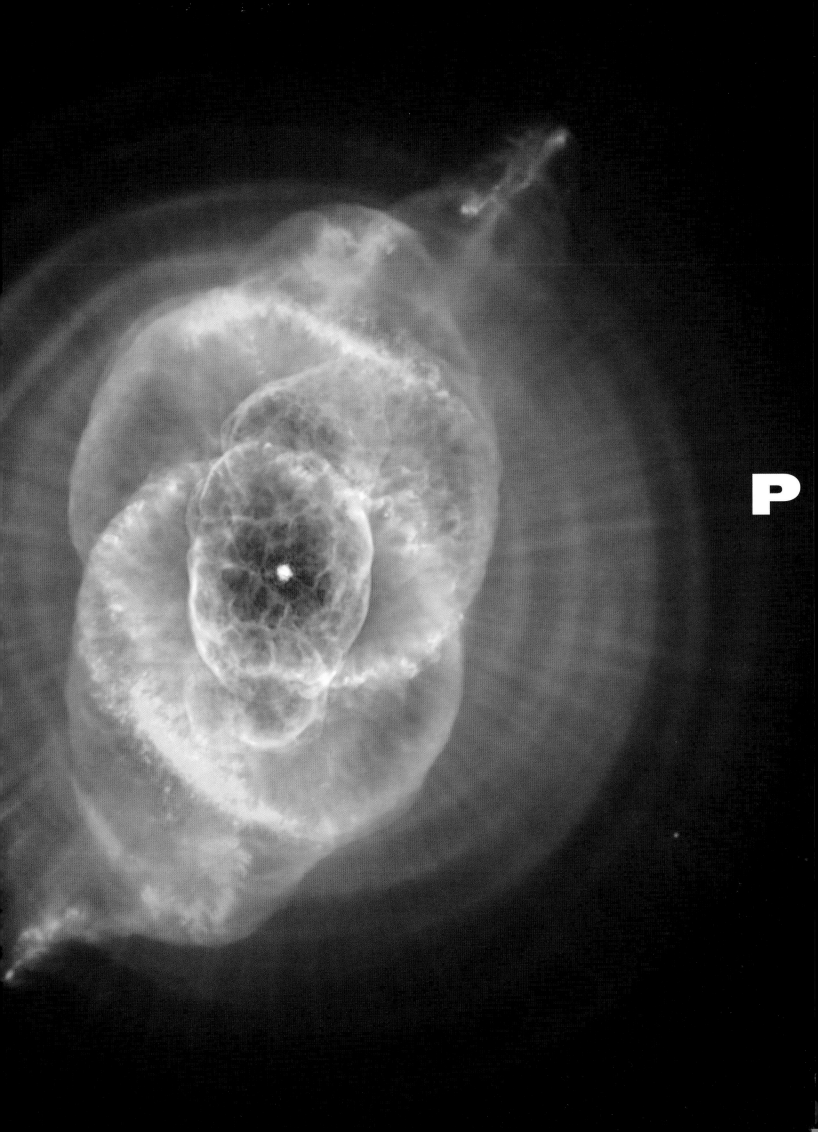

P

PLANET-FORMING DISK

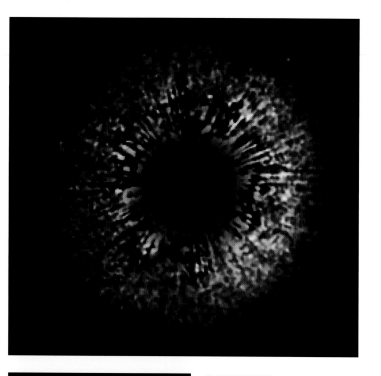

FACE-ON VIEW OF THE
PLANETARY DISK AROUND
THE STAR HD 107146
(BLACK GAP IN MIDDLE)
(RIGHT)

LARGE GAS PLANETS MAY
ALREADY EXIST IN THE DISK.
ROCKY, EARTH-LIKE PLANETS
MAY BE JUST STARTING TO FORM.

VISIBLE-LIGHT IMAGE

HUBBLE SPACE TELESCOPE
(EARTH-ORBITING)

5 JUNE–20 JULY 2004

88 LIGHT-YEARS FROM EARTH

PLANETARY DISK
AROUND AU MICROSCOPII
(LEFT)

THE SPINDLE-SHAPED OBJECT
IS AN EDGE-ON DISK IN THE
FINAL STAGES OF PLANET
FORMATION AROUND A NEWBORN
STAR (BLACK GAP IN MIDDLE)

VISIBLE-LIGHT IMAGE

HUBBLE SPACE TELESCOPE
(EARTH-ORBITING)

3 APRIL 2004

33 LIGHT-YEARS FROM EARTH

THE BIRTH OF PLANETS OFTEN accompanies the birth of stars. A star is born inside a dense nebular cloud of gas and dust. As the star forms, a flat, dusty disk gathers around it in which planets may be born.

This planet-forming disk, composed of tiny grains of matter, is the beginning of a solar system. The grains in the inner disk, where rocky planets form, consist mostly of magnesium, silicon and iron. The grains in the outer disk, where gas giants take shape, are thousands of times more plentiful and are composed mostly of ices – water, ammonia and methane.

These bits collide at low speeds and stick together. As bodies of a mile or more in diameter form, their gravitational pull becomes strong enough to attract more material at an ever increasing rate. In a few million years, a full-blown planet can emerge.

As evolving planets, comets and asteroids circle the star, they crash into one another and shatter. The debris from the impact gathers to form a giant doughnut-shaped disk. The center of this secondary disk may be carved out by orbiting planets. Over time the debris clears, leaving a smaller, more stable disk, similar to the Kuiper Belt in our own outer solar system.

In 2004, the Hubble Space Telescope photographed two such secondary disks, also known as debris disks. The face-on view of the disk at top encircles the Sun-like star HD 107146, which is between 50 and 250 million years old. The red dwarf star at right, AU Microscopii, is only 12 million years old and is surrounded by a disk seen edge on. Both show gaps in the disk where planets may have removed dust and cleared a path.

The sophisticated cloud-piercing instruments on the Spitzer Space Telescope have added greatly to our knowledge of planet formation. In the constellation Centaurus, 13,700 light-years from Earth, Spitzer uncovered the stellar nursery RCW 49 (opposite). Stars harboring planet-forming disks have been confirmed there, and data suggest that 300 or more stars may be construction sites for planets. In 2004, Spitzer surveyed 26 older Sun-like stars known to have planets; six were found to have mature debris disks like that of the Kuiper Belt.

STELLAR NURSERY
IN NEBULA RCW 49
(RIGHT)

INFANT STARS ARE SURROUNDED
BY DUST DISKS THAT MAY
FORM INTO PLANETS

INFRARED IMAGE

SPITZER SPACE TELESCOPE
(EARTH-TRAILING SOLAR ORBIT)

23 DECEMBER 2003

13,700 LIGHT-YEARS FROM EARTH

P

PLUTO

IN GREEK MYTHOLOGY, Pluto was the god of the underworld. This god of darkness was able to make himself invisible. The planet Pluto – the outermost in our solar system – can also be described as dark and elusive.

Pluto has one satellite, Charon, discovered only in 1978. Half the size of Pluto, Charon shares its orbit, and they are sometimes considered a double planet.

Since its discovery in 1930, Pluto has been known as the smallest, coldest and most distant planet from the Sun. However, we know very little about it. No spacecraft has ever visited Pluto, but the New Horizons mission is planned to reach Pluto and its moon Charon in 2015. Since the late 1970s, most of what we know has been learned from ground-based observations, an infrared satellite mission and the Hubble Space Telescope.

We know that Pluto takes 248 years to circle the Sun. We also know that the planet revolves in a peculiar orbit, which is influenced by Neptune. Pluto plays a kind of cat-and-mouse game with Neptune. For a 20-year period during its long, elliptical orbit, Pluto is actually closer to the Sun than Neptune is. The last time

P

that Pluto was in close orbit to the Sun was from 1979 to 1999.

About two-thirds the width of our Moon, Pluto may be composed of a rocky core surrounded by an icy mantle. Its mass is also less than our Moon's. The planet's surface appears to have a bright layer of methane, nitrogen and carbon monoxide. This layer thaws when Pluto moves closer to the Sun.

During the thaw, a fragile atmosphere develops, with pressure of just one-millionth that of Earth's. When Pluto moves away from the Sun, the planet's atmosphere probably freezes and then shrinks as the atmospheric pressure drops, although this is uncertain due to recent observations that seem to indicate Pluto's atmosphere is still growing.

Today some astronomers think that Pluto is among the largest of a group of objects orbiting beyond Neptune in what is called the Kuiper Belt. This belt is filled with small icy bodies of up to 600 miles (1,000km) in size – some of which may be comets – all formed in the early days of our solar system. Some have gone so far as to say that Pluto may not be a planet at all.

PLUTO (LEFT) **WITH ITS MOON, CHARON**
ULTRAVIOLET IMAGE
HUBBLE SPACE TELESCOPE
WITH EUROPEAN
SPACE AGENCY'S FAINT
OBJECT CAMERA
(EARTH-ORBITING)
21 FEBRUARY 1994
2.6 BILLION MILES
(4.4 BILLION KM)
FROM EARTH

PROMINENCE

A PROMINENCE IS A BRIGHT GAS cloud arching outward from the Sun. The term encompasses different types of clouds and flamelike structures that are rooted in the chromosphere and expand into the corona. These ghostly shapes commonly have lower temperatures and higher densities than their surroundings. When such structures are viewed over the edge of the Sun, they appear bright and are known as prominences. When viewed against the Sun's bright disk, they appear dark and are known as filaments.

Think of a prominence as an explosion at a gas station, spewing smoke and flame. The gaseous plumes might be compared to what is known as active prominences. Found in areas of flares and sunspots, active prominences are dynamic, moving in a whirling motion. They can look like a loop, spray or surge shooting tens of thousands of miles off the Sun's surface.

There are other kinds of prominences. Eruptive prominences derive from the same violent origins as coronal mass ejections (charged particles that are expelled when magnetic field lines break and resplice to each other). In fact, many coronal mass ejections are accompanied by eruptive prominences.

Prominences categorized as quiescent are stable structures, lasting weeks or even months, that develop away from the Sun's active regions and along magnetic neutral lines. Quiescent prominences can extend 30,000 miles (50,000km) above the Sun's surface.

P

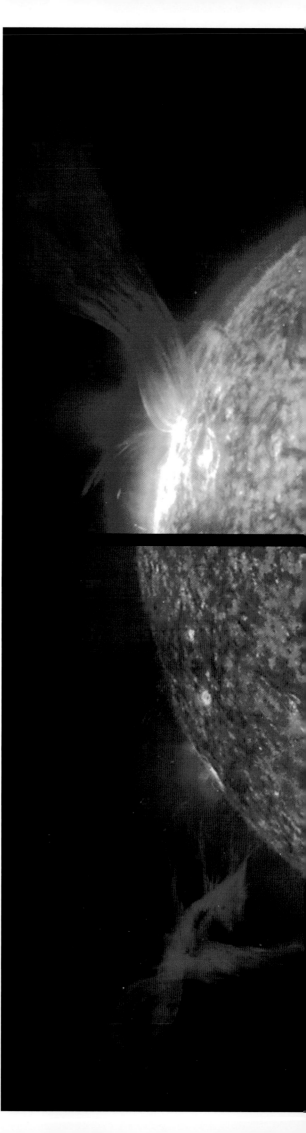

SOLAR PROMINENCES
COLLAGE OF 4 EXTREME- ULTRAVIOLET IMAGES (COLOR ADDED)

EIT TELESCOPE ON SOHO SPACECRAFT

92 MILLION MILES (148 MILLION KM) FROM SOHO

DATES (CLOCKWISE FROM UPPER LEFT): 15 MAY 2001, 28 MARCH 2000, 18 JANUARY 2000, 2 FEBRUARY 2001

93 MILLION MILES (150 MILLION KM) FROM EARTH

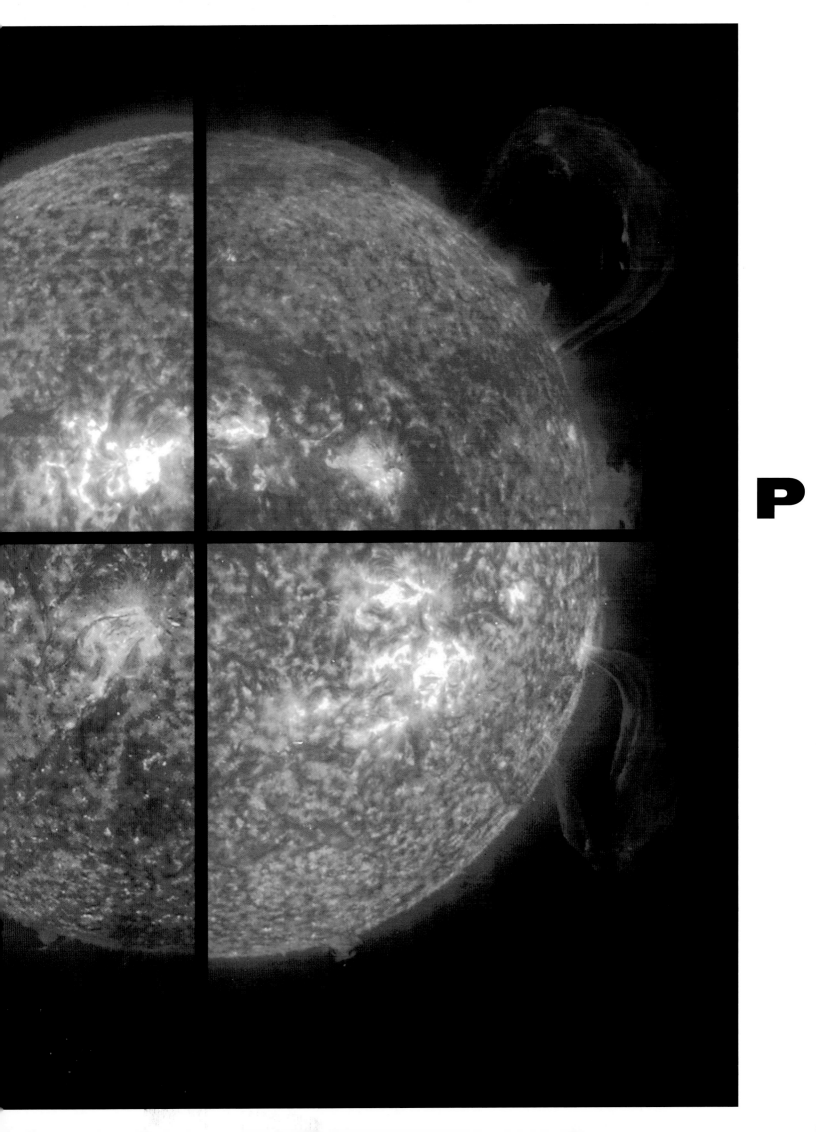

P

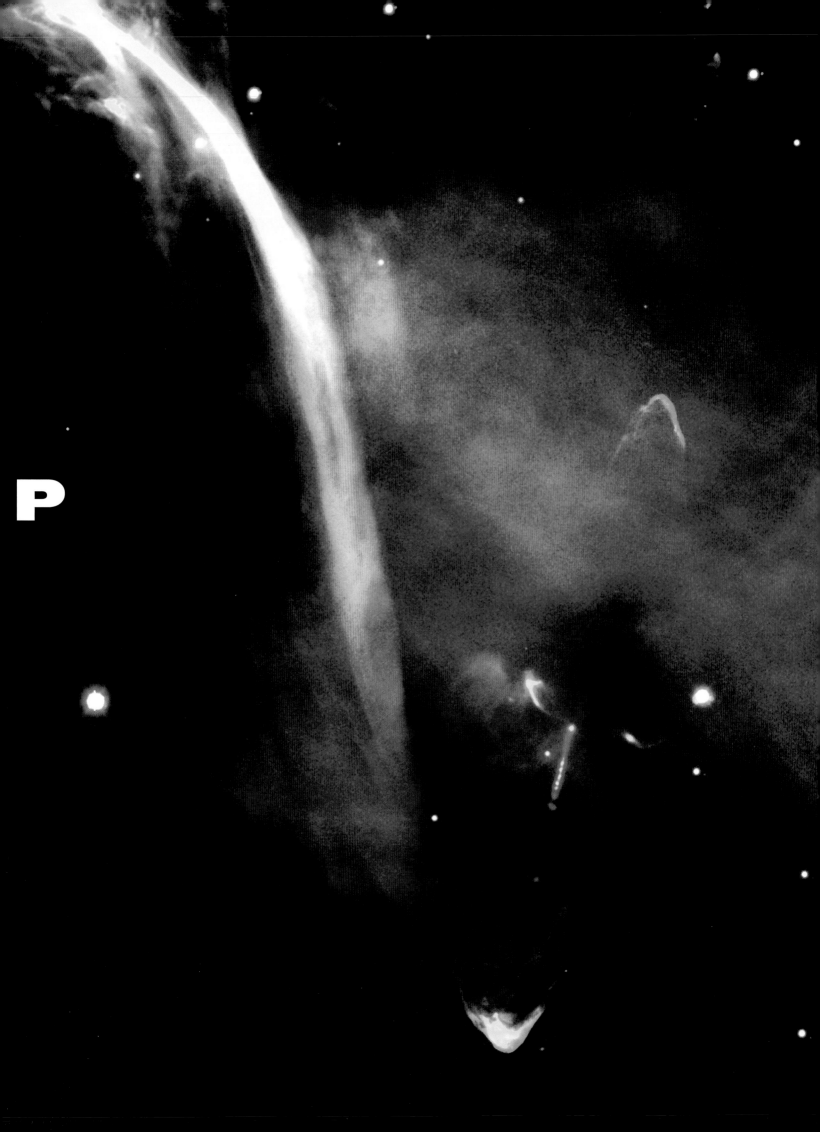

PROTOSTAR

STARS ARE FORMED WHEN DENSE clouds of interstellar matter contract and fragment into increasingly small clumps of matter. Under the force of gravity, the center of a clump forms what is known as a protostar. As the protostar rotates, the remains of the collapsing dust cloud swirl around it, forming a disk.

The protostar grows as material from the disk is drawn or "falls" into it. When large chunks of this material strike the protostar, they release blasts of dense gas called "jets." The jets become visible as they blast their way through the opaque clouds of matter surrounding the embryonic star. And it is the jets seen here (lower center) that reveal the presence of the otherwise invisible protostar.

Protostars generate energy by compressing their gases. As they grow denser and attract more matter, gravitational pull strengthens, the motion of matter increases, and the temperature rises. Nuclear fusion begins when the protostar's core heats up sufficiently for hydrogen to fuse into helium. At this point the protostar becomes a young star.

THE PROTOSTAR STAGE OF HERBIG-HARO OBJECT (HH 34) IN THE CONSTELLATION ORION

JETS OF GAS EMANATE FROM THE PROTOSTAR IN A MACHINE-GUN-LIKE BLAST (LOWER CENTER). THE STAR IS HIDDEN FROM VIEW. THE WATERFALL FEATURE (HH 222) IS UNEXPLAINED.

VISIBLE-LIGHT COMPOSITE THROUGH RED, GREEN AND BLUE FILTERS

EUROPEAN SOUTHERN OBSERVATORY VLT KUEYEN + FORS 2

2 NOVEMBER AND 6 NOVEMBER 1999

1,500 LIGHT-YEARS FROM EARTH

P

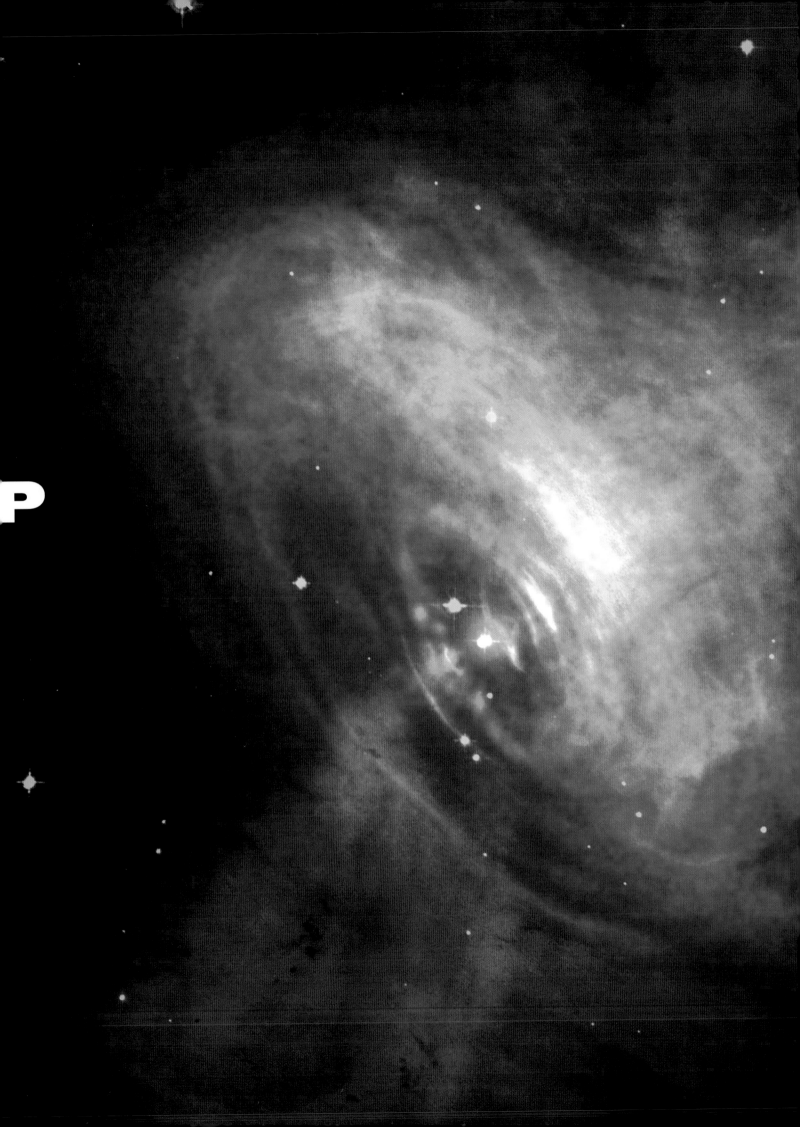

PULSAR

In the aftermath of a super-nova, if the collapsing core of the dying star has too little mass to form a black hole, it becomes a neutron star. It is left spinning furiously, its magnetic field whirling around it. As it rotates, the star sends out beams of radiation, in the form of X-rays, from its magnetic poles.

Some of these neutron stars are called "pulsars," because they emit powerful radio waves in short bursts at regular intervals – like lighthouse beams sweeping through space. Pulsars were discovered in 1967 by radio astronomers.

The pulsar in these images is the bright star in the center of the Crab Nebula, the remains of a supernova recorded by the Chinese in 1054. It sends out pulses 30 times a second.

The composite image at left shows the intense activity around the small star. The rotating pulsar generates a high-speed wind of particles that crash into the nebula, creating a shock wave that forms the inner ring. The shock sends the high-energy particles outward to form the bright outer ring. As shown in the four comparison pictures at right, both the nebula and the pulsar radiate strongly in multiple wavelengths.

P

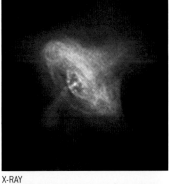

X-RAY

VISIBLE

INFRARED

RADIO

A PULSAR INSIDE THE CRAB NEBULA

A SUPERNOVA REMNANT IN THE CONSTELLATION TAURUS (LEFT)

COMPOSITE OF X-RAY AND VISIBLE-LIGHT IMAGES

CHANDRA X-RAY OBSERVATORY/ HUBBLE SPACE TELESCOPE (EARTH-ORBITING)

25 NOVEMBER 2000– 6 APRIL 2001

6,000 LIGHT-YEARS FROM EARTH

MULTIWAVELENGTH COMPARISON
(FOUR IMAGES AT RIGHT)

X-RAY: CHANDRA X-RAY OBSERVATORY

VISIBLE: PALOMAR OBSERVATORY

INFRARED: 2MASS

RADIO: VLA/NRAO

RED GIANT

WHEN THE MAIN STAGE OF LIFE ends, all stars become red giants or – in the case of the most massive stars – red supergiants. Throughout their long and stable maturity, stars generate radiation by nuclear fusion, as heat at the core fuses hydrogen into helium. It is when the core's hydrogen is depleted that the star becomes a red giant.

At this point the core contracts, while the star itself expands, burning the hydrogen in its outer atmosphere. As the red giant grows larger, its surface cools. The core, however, contracts and becomes hotter. When the core is down to one-tenth of its former size, the temperature becomes high enough to burn helium. Nuclear fusion now resumes, and with helium fueling the core, the temperature on the surface also rises. Eventually, the helium too is exhausted.

Once the helium is gone, the most massive stars – where the core has burned intensely enough to fuse carbon and oxygen – collapse on themselves and explode, creating a supernova. This will be the fate of red supergiant Betelgeuse, shown here. One of the brightest stars in the constellation Orion, it is a thousand times the size of our Sun.

Stars the size of our Sun do not create supernovas, but their exit is surely dramatic enough. When the Sun becomes a red giant, in about five billion years, it will expand thirty or more times and become a thousand times brighter. It will consume Mercury, and possibly Venus as well. Eventually, when its helium is gone, the core will collapse into a white dwarf.

**THE RED SUPERGIANT
BETELGEUSE
(ALPHA ORIONIS) IN THE
CONSTELLATION ORION**

THE FIRST DIRECT IMAGE
OF A STAR'S DISK OTHER
THAN THAT OF THE SUN

VISIBLE-LIGHT IMAGE

HUBBLE SPACE TELESCOPE
(EARTH-ORBITING)

3 MARCH 1995

600 LIGHT-YEARS
FROM EARTH

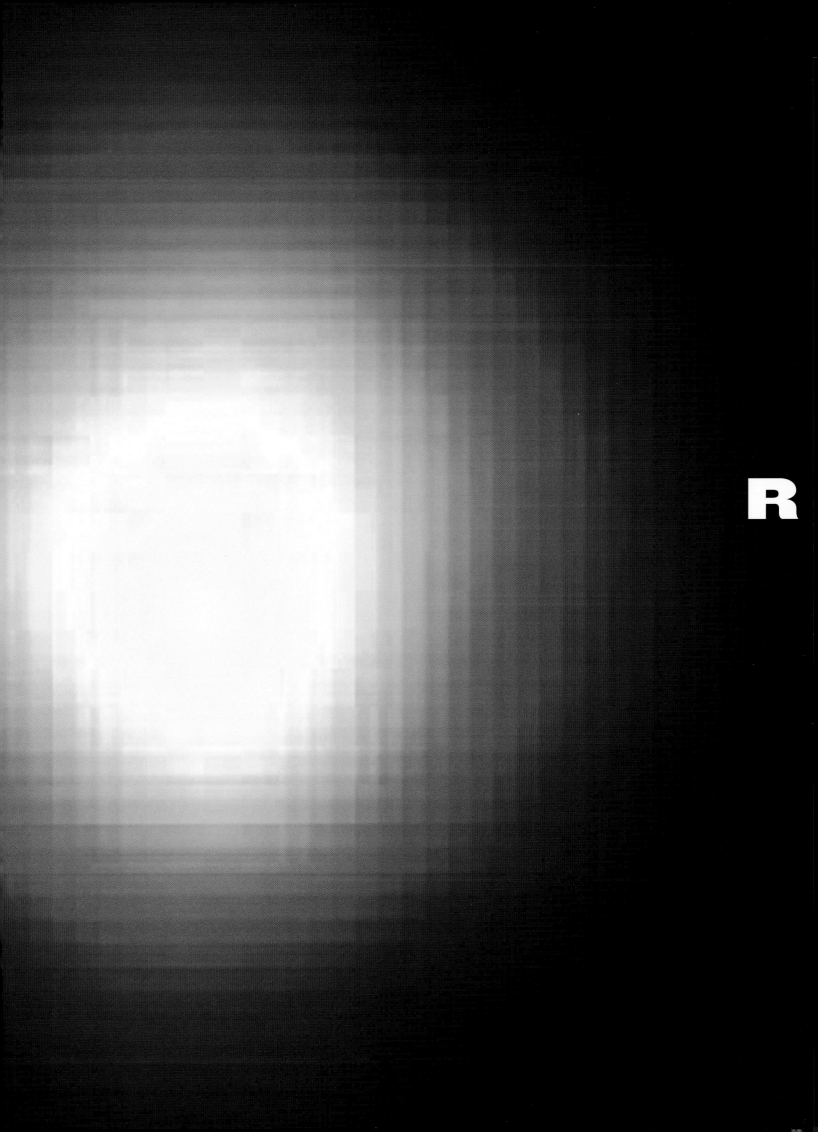

R

REFLECTION NEBULA

R

WHILE EMISSION NEBULAS generate their own light, reflection nebulas are dependent on the illumination of stars. These nebulas are visible from Earth only when there is light from nearby stars for them to reflect. In an effect known as scattering, the bright light of the star is deflected off the nebula's dust. Reflection nebulas are usually blue, because blue light is more readily deflected than red.

Illuminated by bright stars, the blue reflection nebulas at left are located in the Chamaeleon constellation, which is visible in the skies of the Southern Hemisphere roughly between January and May. Reflection nebulas, like emission nebulas, are often the site of star birth. In the thick dust of the dark molecular clouds toward the top and lower right, new stars are being born. At 450 light-years from Earth, this complex is one of the closest star hatcheries.

What we see in the large image is the fragility of nebulas. Here, radiation from the star Merope, one of the brightest in the Pleiades cluster, illuminates a reflection nebula while destroying it. As the star cluster drifts through the nebula, the nebula is being torn apart by radiation from Merope.

REFLECTION NEBULAS IN THE CONSTELLATION CHAMAELEON

THE COLORFUL NEBULAS CONTAIN SMALL DUST PARTICLES THAT REFLECT THE LIGHT OF THE STARS THAT ILLUMINATE THEM. THE BRIGHT STAR AT THE CENTER HAS TWICE THE MASS OF OUR SUN.

VISIBLE-LIGHT IMAGE

EUROPEAN SOUTHERN OBSERVATORY
8.2M VLT ANTU

JANUARY 1999

450 LIGHT-YEARS FROM EARTH

BARNARD'S MEROPE (NEBULA IC 349) IN THE PLEIADES STAR CLUSTER

A REFLECTION NEBULA LIT BY RADIATION FROM THE STAR MEROPE (OUTSIDE OF THE IMAGE, UPPER RIGHT)

VISIBLE-LIGHT IMAGE

HUBBLE SPACE TELESCOPE (EARTH-ORBITING)

19 SEPTEMBER 1999

380 LIGHT-YEARS FROM EARTH

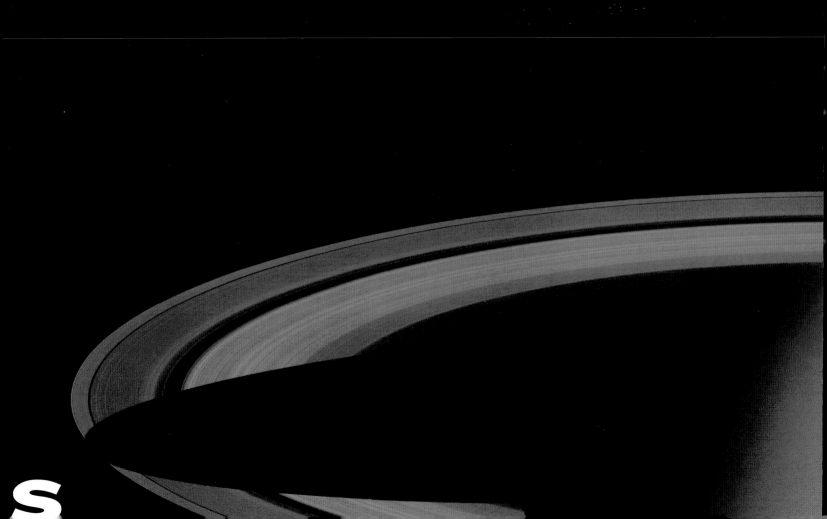

S

the warmest place on the planet. Atmospheric pressure is sufficient to cause Saturn's gases to condense into a sea of liquid hydrogen about 250 miles (400km) below the cloud tops. The planet's density is the lowest in the solar system, its specific gravity less than that of water; if there were an ocean large enough to contain it, the planet would float.

The atmosphere is com-posed of three layers of clouds – white, orange and blue – and capped with a thick layer of haze. Storms more forceful than Jupiter's occasionally climb through the haze and appear as white clouds of ammonia ice. Winds in the upper atmosphere reach speeds as high as 1,100 mph (1,800kph) as they whirl around the equator. The winds, in combination with the heat rising from the planet's interior, account for the yellow and gold bands visible in Saturn's atmo-sphere. The synergy of high-speed rotation and the planet's gaseous makeup produces its characteristic flat poles and a bulging equator, the plumpest in the solar system.

In 2004, after a two-billion-mile, seven-year journey, the Cassini-Huygens spacecraft entered Saturn's orbit to give the planet its close-ups.

SATURN IN NATURAL COLOR
VISIBLE-LIGHT MOSAIC OF 126 IMAGES
CASSINI ORBITER
3.9 MILLION MILES (6.3 MILLION KM) FROM CASSINI
6 OCTOBER 2004
.9 BILLION MILES (1.4 BILLION KM) FROM EARTH

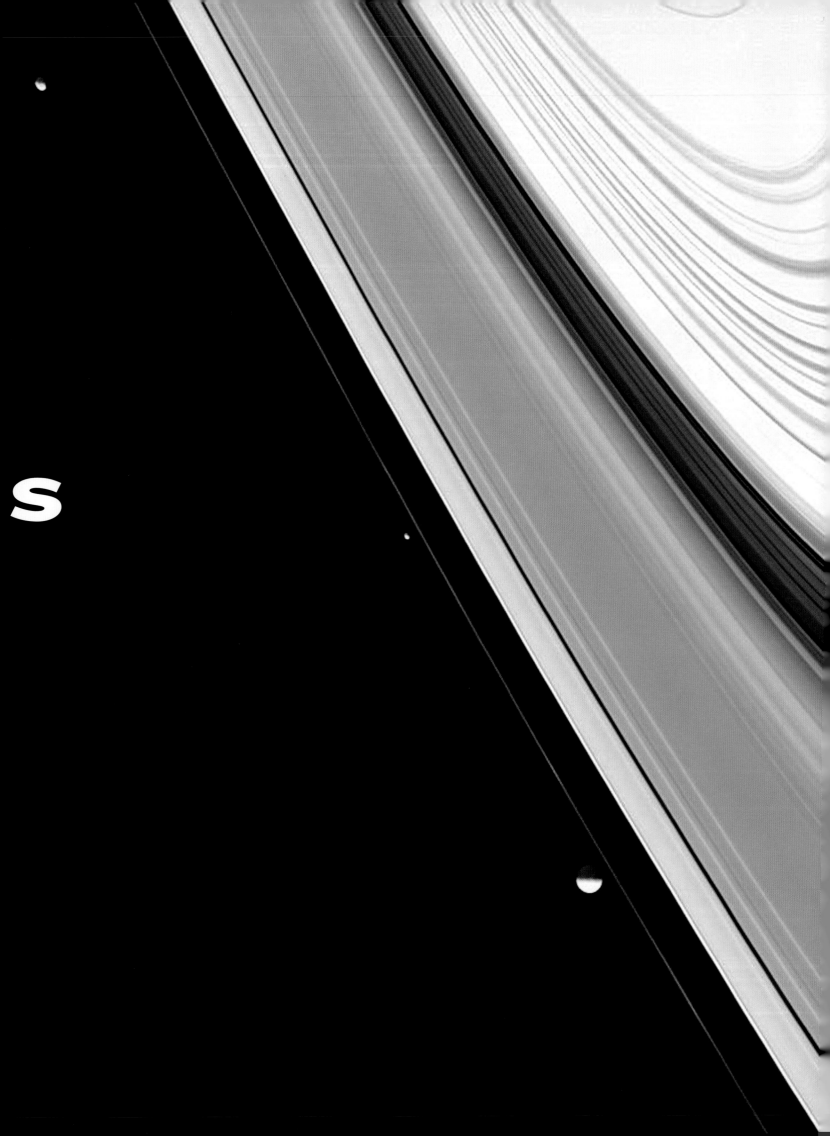

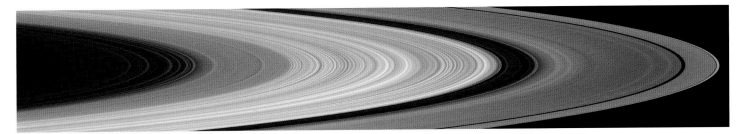

SATURN: THE RINGS

Saturn's ringscape is like a mini-solar system where the planet, moons and ring particles are balanced in a collaborative display. The inner satellites play a key role as they choreograph particles to clear gaps, create waves and form ringlets.

Even though there are a multitude of ringlets, the ring plane is divided into seven main rings designated by letters — D, C, B, A, F, G and E in order from the planet. The closer rings orbit Saturn at faster speeds. Density waves within the rings are the result of nearby passing moons. The revolving moons disturb the orbits of particles, and density waves are formed as particles move closer together.

The Cassini Division between the B and A rings is the largest apparent interruption in Saturn's grooves. The inner boundary is formed by particles located on the outer edge of the B ring. They orbit Saturn twice for every time the moon Mimas goes around the planet once. This process is called orbital resonance.

One of the smaller gaps, the Encke Division, is located in the outer portion of the A ring and is formed by the orbital path of the tiny moon Pan. Pan acts like a rotating broom sweeping away debris as it moves through the gap, causing ropelike braids and wakes along Encke's edges.

Satellites Prometheus and Pandora perform a different role by shepherding the F ring into a narrow strand. Prometheus is on the inside of the ring, Pandora on the outside. The gravitational forces of the moons corral any material trying to escape.

RINGS AND MOONS
(LEFT)
THREE OF SATURN'S MOONS BEYOND THE F RING — JANUS (TOP), PANDORA (CENTER) AND MIMAS (BOTTOM)
VISIBLE-LIGHT IMAGE
CASSINI ORBITER
1.7 MILLION MILES (2.7 MILLION KM) FROM CASSINI
22 JANUARY 2005
.75 BILLION MILES (1.2 BILLION KM) FROM EARTH

PANORAMA OF RINGS
(TOP)
VARIATIONS, GAPS, GRAVITATIONAL RESONANCES AND WAVE PATTERNS ARE REVEALED IN SATURN'S MOST STRIKING FEATURE
VISIBLE-LIGHT MOSAIC
CASSINI ORBITER
1.1 MILLION MILES (1.8 MILLION KM) FROM CASSINI
12 DECEMBER 2004

DARK SIDE OF THE RINGS
(ABOVE)
RINGS ARE ILLUMINATED FROM BELOW BY THE SUN. DENSE AND EMPTY REGIONS APPEAR DARK. REGIONS OF MEDIUM PARTICLE DENSITY APPEAR BRIGHT.
VISIBLE-LIGHT IMAGE
CASSINI ORBITER
588,000 MILES (946,000KM) FROM CASSINI
14 DECEMBER 2004

A SAMPLER OF
SATURN'S MOONS

DIONE

ENCELADUS

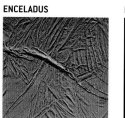

HYPERION

IAPETUS

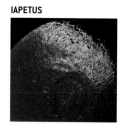

MIMAS

PHOEBE

S

RHEA

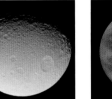

TETHYS

TITAN

MONOCHROMATIC MOON DIONE AGAINST THE BACKGROUND OF SATURN
(LEFT)

VISIBLE-LIGHT IMAGE

CASSINI ORBITER

375,000 MILES (603,000KM) FROM CASSINI TO DIONE

14 DECEMBER 2004

.75 BILLION MILES (1.2 BILLION KM) FROM EARTH

THE MOON MIMAS AGAINST SATURN'S NORTHERN HEMISPHERE
(ABOVE)

SHADOWS OF THE RINGS STREAK SATURN'S SURFACE. THE BRIGHT BLUE STREAK ABOVE MIMAS IS SUNLIGHT PASSING THROUGH THE CASSINI DIVISION. THE TRANSPARENT A RING APPEARS AT THE BOTTOM.

VISIBLE-LIGHT IMAGE

CASSINI ORBITER

2.3 MILLION MILES (3.7 MILLION KM) FROM CASSINI

7 NOVEMBER 2004

.8 BILLION MILES (1.3 BILLION KM) FROM EARTH

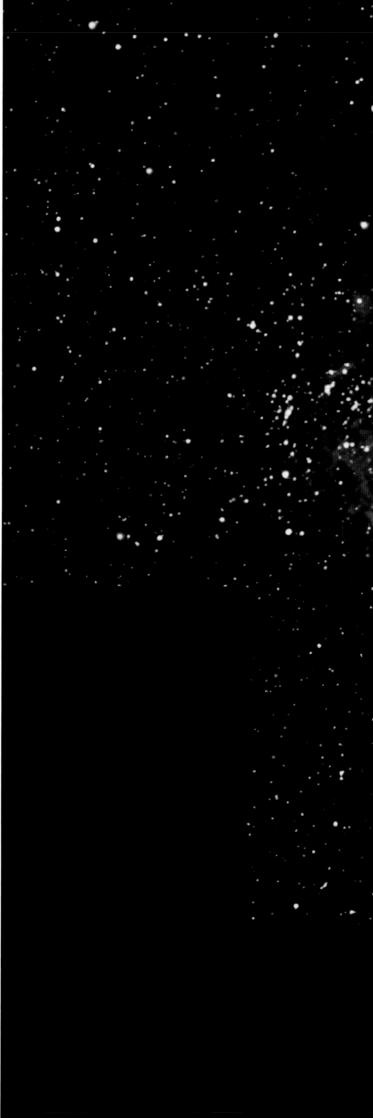

STAR

s

HUMANITY HAS ALWAYS BEEN fascinated by stars. In antiquity, people thought they were holes in the roof of the world. Through them, they believed, one could see fires burning outside. To the ancient Greeks, anything in the sky, other than the Sun and the Moon, was called a star. Planets were "wandering stars" and comets "stars with hair."

Stars, of course, are suns – like our Sun – balls of gas that generate energy and emit radiation. They come in a wide range of sizes, but all lie within an upper and lower weight limit on the stellar scale. Red dwarf stars, for example, can have less than one-tenth the mass of our Sun. That's about as lightweight as a star can be for nuclear fusion to occur in its core and starshine to come about. Most stars in our galaxy are red dwarfs.

Blue supergiants are the heavyweights, at the upper end of the scale. Scientists suspect that blue supergiants actually have a weight limit no more than 150 times the mass of our Sun.

For a star, its mass – the amount of matter it contains – determines its destiny. The greater the mass, the hotter and brighter it burns. And temperature dictates color. The hottest stars (above 45,000 °F/ 25,000 °C) are blue. Blue supergiants are even hotter because they burn hydrogen at a faster rate. The coolest stars (below 6,000 °F/ 3,200 °C) are red. Others are yellow, like our Sun. Mass also determines

THE FIRESTORM NEBULA (NGC 604)

THE LARGEST KNOWN CAULDRON OF STAR BIRTH

VISIBLE-LIGHT IMAGE

HUBBLE SPACE TELESCOPE (EARTH-ORBITING)

JULY 1994, JANUARY 1995, DECEMBER 2001

2.7 MILLION LIGHT-YEARS FROM EARTH

S

s

the length of a star's life cycle. The more massive the star, the faster it burns and the more quickly it consumes itself. So stars that keep cool live longer by burning slower.

An infant star begins life in the cold and dark. Birthing occurs within globules, dense clouds of hydrogen found in nebulas. Under the force of gravity, the globule shrinks and collapses, creating what are known as protostars. The protostar continues to contract until the heat and pressure are intense enough to set off nuclear fusion. It is now a star.

The protostar stage is only a small fraction of the total life of the star. Once mature, stars remain stable for most of their lives. Nuclear fusion – converting hydrogen to helium in the star's hot core – releases vast amounts of energy. But, eventually, the core's hydrogen is depleted. Nuclear fusion subsides. The core contracts and the star enlarges, burning the hydrogen in its outer atmosphere. It becomes a red giant. Nuclear fusion resumes and changes from burning hydrogen to burning helium.

What happens when all the helium is consumed is again a question of mass. Massive stars collapse in on themselves, lighting up the sky in gigantic explosions called supernovas.

The fate of the core also depends on mass. Stars with the most massive cores implode to form black holes, regions of immense gravitational pull. Less massive cores become neutron stars, with a diameter of only about 12 miles (19km)

S

but of unimaginable density.

Modest stars like our medium-size Sun never get hot enough for such a flashy end. The gas and dust are released to form a planetary nebula that eventually disperses. The core contracts to a white dwarf — a small, dense star about the size of Earth with a mass like the Sun's. In time, when its remaining energy is spent, it literally fades away.

A STELLAR NURSERY IN THE DR 21 REGION OF THE CONSTELLATION CYGNUS

INFRARED LIGHT SEES INSIDE A SHROUD OF DUST TO CAPTURE MASSIVE STARS BEING BORN

COMPOSITE OF INFRARED AND VISIBLE-LIGHT IMAGES

SPITZER SPACE TELESCOPE (EARTH-TRAILING SOLAR ORBIT)

11 OCTOBER AND 22 NOVEMBER 2003

6,200 LIGHT-YEARS FROM EARTH

SUN

In the grand scheme of things, the Sun is just an ordinary, medium-size yellow star located on an arm of the Milky Way Galaxy. The Milky Way is but one of about 150 billion galaxies in the universe. Earth and eight other planets orbit the Sun. And the Sun carries them along, at 150 miles (240km) per second, as it travels on an orbit of its own within the Milky Way – a trip that takes 225 million years.

As stars go, the Sun may be no more than average size. But to us here on Earth, it is immense. One million Earths could fit into the Sun, which has a diameter of 864,000 miles (1,390,000km). It makes up 99 percent of our solar system's mass.

Life on Earth is absolutely dependent on the Sun. It is the heart of the solar system, the source of all energy, heat and light. So what would happen if the Sun suddenly shut down? Light from the Sun, which is 93 million miles (150 million km) away, travels to Earth in a matter of eight minutes. If this light were extinguished, it would take eight minutes for our world to be plunged into total darkness. Since the Sun warms our planet, all animal and plant life would be thrown into a terminal deep freeze.

It is estimated that the Sun was formed 4.6 billion years ago, when our solar system was just a cloud of gas, dust and ice. Gravity caused the cloud to shrink and form into a gaseous sphere. The inner part, or center, became the Sun, while the outer part became our planets.

As our solar system evolved, Earth reached an almost solid state. The Sun, however, is still made up of gases. It is composed largely of hydrogen (92.1 percent), with some helium (7.8 percent) and a trace of heavier elements (0.1 percent).

The Sun's energy comes from nuclear fusion. Heat and pressure at the center force

SUN COMPOSITE

THREE IMAGES COMBINED TO HIGH-LIGHT DIFFERENT TEMPERATURE RANGES (SEPARATE RED, GREEN AND BLUE IMAGES ON FOLLOWING PAGES)

EXTREME-ULTRAVIOLET IMAGE (COLOR ADDED)

EIT TELESCOPE ON SOHO SPACECRAFT

92 MILLION MILES (148 MILLION KM) FROM SOHO

29 MAY 1998

93 MILLION MILES (150 MILLION KM) FROM EARTH

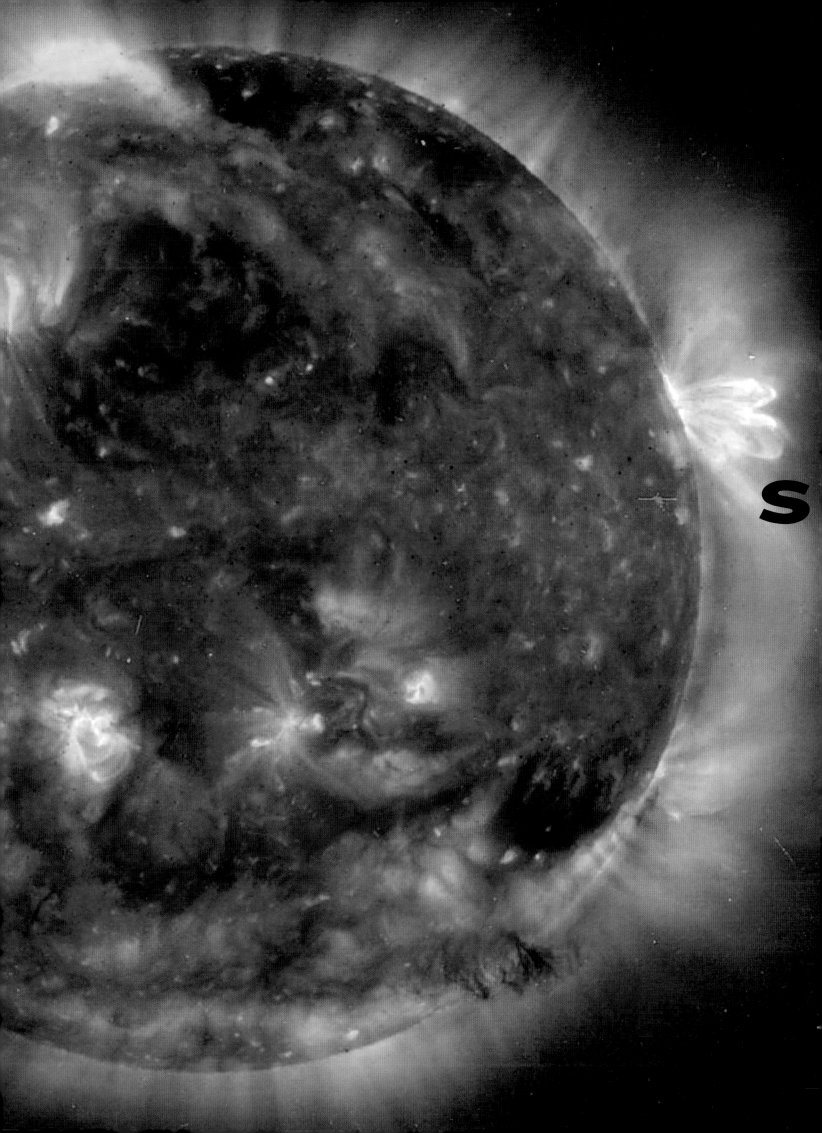

hydrogen atoms together. This condition starts a reaction that fuses the hydrogen nuclei and creates helium atoms. The process releases unfathomable amounts of energy and is not unlike the explosion of a hydrogen bomb.

The energy the Sun produces comes to us as light, which travels from the Sun to Earth in waves of electromagnetic radiation. And the electromagnetic spectrum contains light of every different wavelength. Some light is visible and can be seen with an optical telescope. The rest is invisible: gamma rays, X-rays, ultraviolet, infrared, microwaves and radio waves. Special telescopes can detect this invisible radiation.

But the Sun is more than a nuclear furnace, predictably producing energy. Its sometimes erratic behavior is determined by electromagnetic activity. Like Earth, the Sun has a main magnetic field with opposite north and south magnetic poles. Earth's field is formed by the movement of molten iron within our planet's superheated core. The Sun's field is formed by the movement of electrically charged particles called plasma — a mixture of positively charged nuclei and free electrons that have been separated by the tremendous heat and radiation of the Sun's interior.

There is a cycle to the magnetic activity of the Sun. It starts with magnetic field lines (invisible lines of force) running neatly from pole to pole. But since the Sun rotates more rapidly at its equator than at its poles, the magnetic field lines tend to stretch. The flow of plasma drags these field lines about, creating new currents and producing more magnetic fields. Thus magnetic activity varies from one region of the Sun to another. Activity rises and falls. It peaks, wanes and

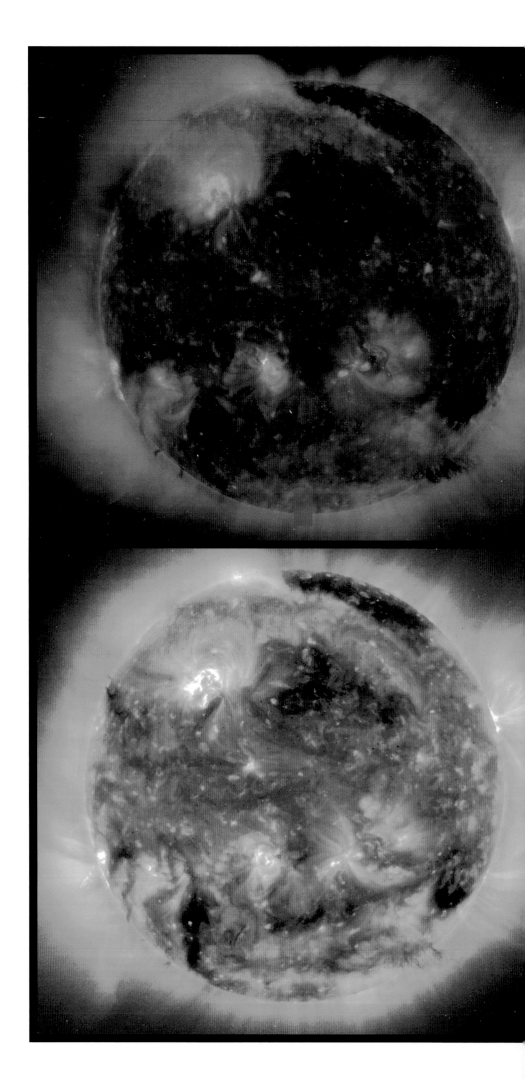

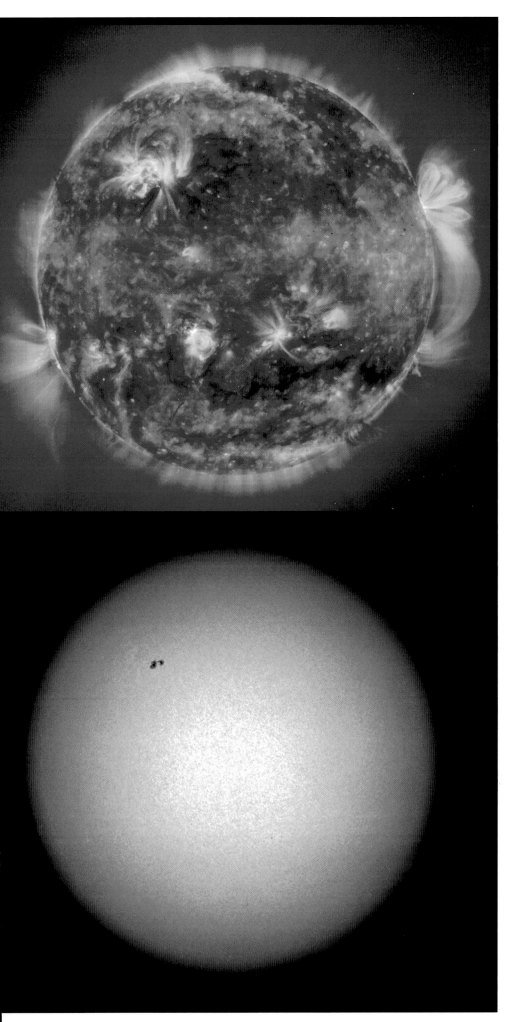

peaks again over the course of a cycle that lasts an average of 11 years.

It is the shifting of magnetic fields that causes electrical storms in the Sun's outer atmosphere, making the corona – the halo around the Sun – hundreds of times hotter than the underlying visible surface of the Sun called the photosphere. Magnetic field lines in the Sun's core twist and rise into the corona as loops. The volatile loops snap and reconnect with other loops, releasing energy and producing the dramatic solar events known as flares and coronal mass ejections (CMEs).

Eventually, the Sun will shut down. The hydrogen will burn out and the Sun will begin to burn helium, increasing in luminosity as well as in size. Temperatures will rise in our solar system. Once the helium is gone, the Sun will explode. Its core will collapse into a white dwarf star about the size of Earth. All this will happen in about five billion years.

THE ULTRAVIOLET SUN
THREE IMAGES THAT HIGHLIGHT
THE SUN'S TEMPERATURE RANGES
(COMPOSITE ON PREVIOUS PAGE)
TOP LEFT: INNER CORONA
TOP RIGHT: LOWER INNER CORONA
BOTTOM LEFT: UPPER TRANSITION
REGION BETWEEN THE CHROMOSPHERE
AND THE CORONA
EXTREME-ULTRAVIOLET IMAGES
(COLOR ADDED)
EIT TELESCOPE ON SOHO SPACECRAFT
92 MILLION MILES
(148 MILLION KM) FROM SOHO
29 MAY 1998
93 MILLION MILES
(150 MILLION KM) FROM EARTH

THE VISIBLE SUN
(BOTTOM RIGHT)
PHOTOSPHERE IN VISIBLE LIGHT
MDI TELESCOPE ON SOHO SPACECRAFT
29 MAY 1998

SUNSPOT

S

A SUNSPOT LOOKS LIKE A BLACK patch on the Sun's luminous, visible surface, the photosphere. However, the dark spot is not totally devoid of light.

Sunspots happen where the Sun's magnetic field suppresses light and heat from the area it surrounds. When giant bundles of magnetic field lines emerge from inside the Sun as coronal loops, their imposing presence inhibits the flow of heat. These spots punctuate where the field is strongest, resulting in a cooler surface

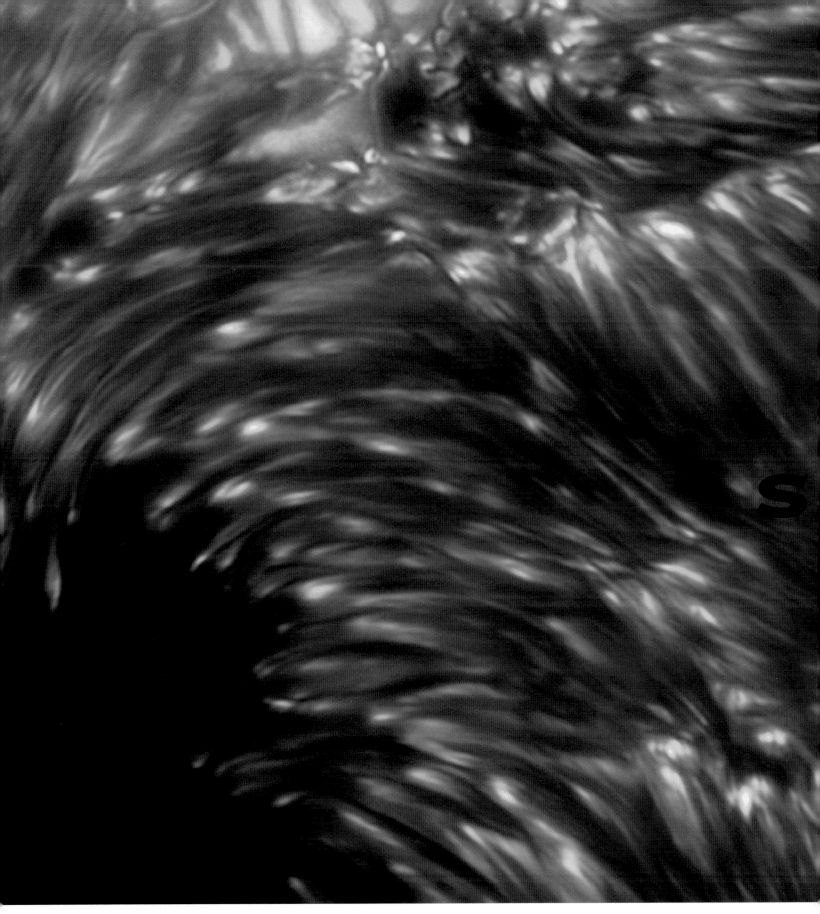

area – apparent in visible-light images as a sunspot. The middle of the spot, called the umbra, looks black because it is a thousand or more degrees cooler than the neighboring photosphere, which is about 10,000°F (5,500°C).

There is an average 11-year sunspot cycle that is influenced by the Sun reversing its overall magnetic polarity. If a compass could survive on the Sun, the needle would switch from north to south. During this period, the number of visible sunspots goes from a maximum to a minimum and back to a maximum again. At the height of the cycle, 150 sunspots may be visible in a single sunrise-to-sunset period. Sunspots often appear in pairs of opposite magnetic polarity.

SUNSPOT IN ACTIVE REGION 10030
VISIBLE-LIGHT IMAGE (COLOR ADDED)
SWEDISH 1M SOLAR TELESCOPE
15 JULY 2002
93 MILLION MILES (150 MILLION KM) FROM EARTH

SUPERNOVA

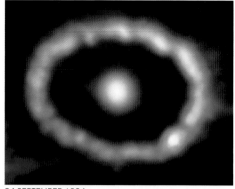

24 SEPTEMBER 1994

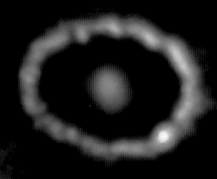

10 JULY 1997

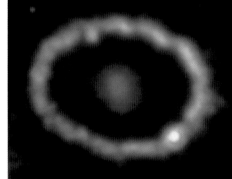

6 FEBRUARY 1998

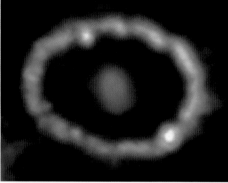

8 JANUARY 1999

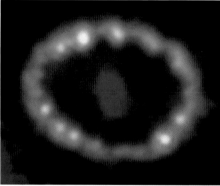

7 DECEMBER 2001

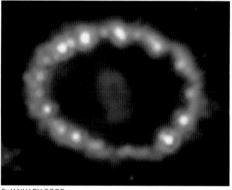

5 JANUARY 2003

S

A NOVA IS A STAR THAT HAS A temporary burst of activity and increased brightness. Early astronomers, believing they were seeing a new star, used the Latin word "nova," meaning new. A supernova is a super-burst of light, but rather than a beginning it announces the cataclysmic explosion of a star at the end of its life cycle.

There are two types of supernovas. One type involves a white dwarf in a binary system with a larger star. The white dwarf pulls in matter from its companion star. When the white dwarf can no longer sustain itself it collapses, setting off a thermonuclear explosion, or supernova.

Most supernovas, however, are massive stars that have consumed all their own available fuel. In this kind of core-collapse supernova, the star's core shrinks. It gets denser and hotter – hot enough to fuse oxygen and carbon into heavier elements. Eventually, the core is solid iron, and its enormous mass causes it to collapse – in about one second. So much

energy is released that the star blasts into space. In the aftermath, the core becomes a neutron star or a black hole, depending on its mass.

Core-collapse supernovas produce incredible shock waves, sending the star's outer layers into space at speeds up to 12,500 miles (20,100km) a second. This violent ejection of matter leads to the fusion of heavy chemical elements. In fact, all elements heavier than iron in the universe were created by supernovas. These materials eventually regroup in nebulas, where new stars are born.

The images here show a ring of gaseous matter as it is illumi-

nated by shock waves emanating from a supernova. While it was first spotted in 1987 – the brightest supernova seen from Earth in 400 years – the star actually exploded 160,000 years ago, the time it has taken for its light to reach us.

Supernovas are very rare in our galaxy. Only one supernova goes off every century in the Milky Way. But the universe is so rich in galaxies that astronomers calculate that a supernova goes off somewhere every second.

A RING OF GAS EXCITED BY A SUPERNOVA SHOCK WAVE IN THE LARGE MAGELLANIC CLOUD

VISIBLE-LIGHT IMAGE

HUBBLE SPACE TELESCOPE (EARTH-ORBITING)

24 SEPTEMBER 1994– 28 NOVEMBER 2003

160,000 LIGHT-YEARS FROM EARTH

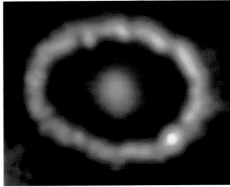

5 MARCH 1995

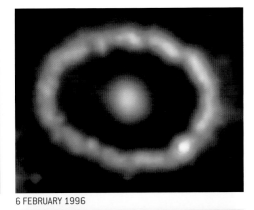

6 FEBRUARY 1996

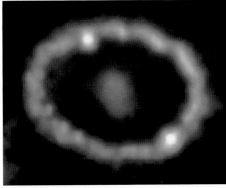

2 FEBRUARY 2000

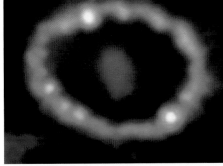

16 JUNE 2000

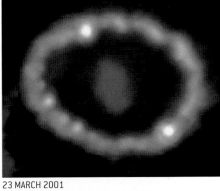

23 MARCH 2001

s

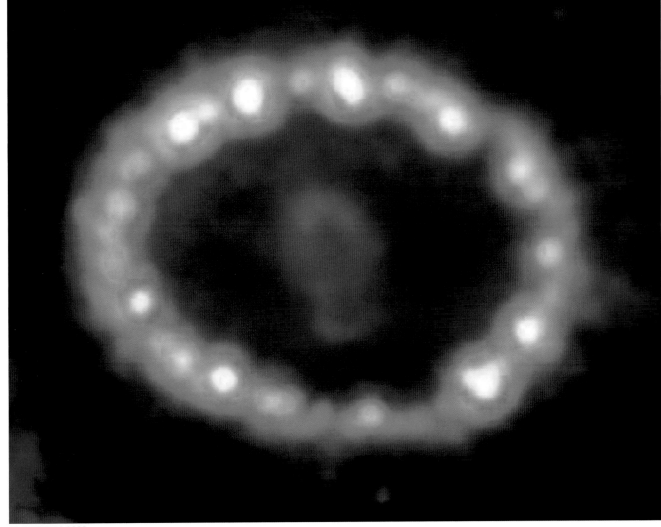

28 NOVEMBER 2003

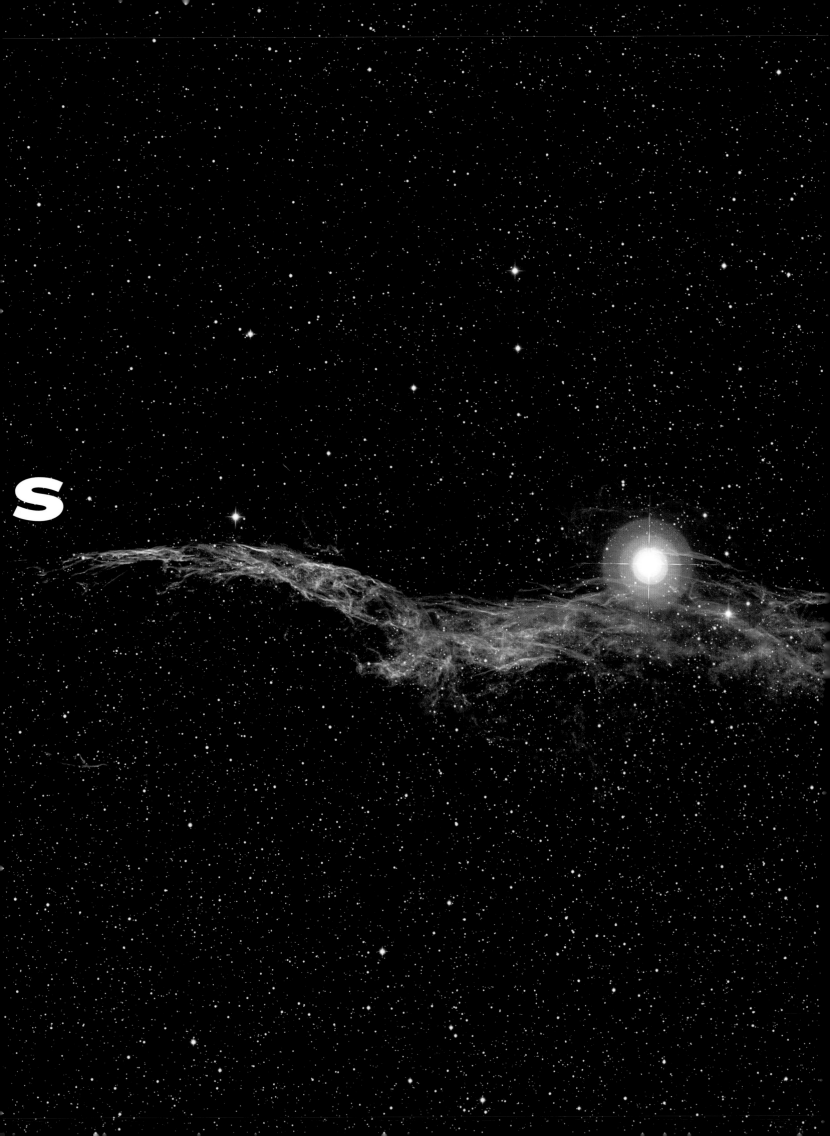

s

SUPERNOVA REMNANT

THE BIGGER THE STAR, THE HARDER it falls. And blue supergiants — the biggest, brightest and hottest stars in the sky — fall hardest of all. When these stars have exhausted their hydrogen and burned away their helium, the core collapses until it releases a vast wave of energy, a supernova that blasts apart the remnants of the star and releases a mass of newly formed elements. The expanding shell of gas and dust that remains after this cataclysmic explosion is called a supernova remnant (SNR). It carries within it the heavy elements fused in the star's core and dispersed when the core blew apart.

The SNR begins a journey through the interstellar medium, transporting materials that will be used to spawn a new generation of stars. All elements heavier than iron, including gold, are carried along by SNRs. Such elements are critical to the creation of rocky planets. Some evidence suggests that a shock wave from a supernova explosion four-and-a-half billion years ago triggered the formation of our own solar system.

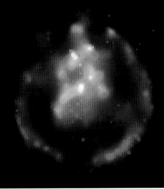

SUPERNOVA REMNANT SNR 0103-72.6 IN THE SMALL MAGELLANIC CLOUD (TOP)

THE PRESENCE OF OXYGEN AND NEON PROVE THAT THE EXPLODING STAR WAS 10 TIMES AS MASSIVE AS OUR SUN

X-RAY IMAGE

CHANDRA X-RAY OBSERVATORY (EARTH-ORBITING)

27 AUGUST 2002

190,000 LIGHT-YEARS FROM EARTH

VEIL NEBULA (NGC 6960) (LEFT)

THIS WISPY NEBULA IS THE SHATTERED REMAINS OF ONE OR POSSIBLY TWO SUPERNOVAS THAT EXPLODED 15,000 YEARS AGO

VISIBLE-LIGHT IMAGE THROUGH 3 FILTERS (REPRESENTATIVE COLOR)

NSF 0.9M TELESCOPE AT KITT PEAK NATIONAL OBSERVATORY, NOAO

14 SEPTEMBER 2000

1,400 LIGHT-YEARS FROM EARTH

TITAN

The secrets of Titan, Saturn's largest moon, have long been guarded by its dense atmosphere. But on 14 January 2005, the Huygens probe parachuted down through Titan's thick haze.

As it descended, Huygens transmitted data back to its mother ship, the Cassini orbiter, which had carried it on its seven-year journey to the Saturn system. Huygens (named for the Dutch astronomer Christiaan Huygens, who discovered Titan in 1655) captured images, sampled the atmosphere and reported climatic conditions. It made a soft landing on a sand-like area, bathed in light from Titan's distinctive orange sky. Its main mission accomplished, Huygens continued transmitting information for 72 minutes before Cassini disappeared below the horizon.

Named after the race of giant gods who ruled the heavens in Greek mythology, Titan was once thought to be the largest satellite in the solar system. At 3,200 miles (5,500km) in diameter, however, it is actually second in size to Jupiter's Ganymede, though it is still bigger than the planet Mercury. Titan circles Saturn every 16 days at a distance of about 753,000 miles (1.2 million km).

What makes Titan unique is that it is the only moon in the solar system known to have a dense, planetlike atmosphere. It also has surface features that bear a striking resemblance to Earth. River channels appear carved into the landscape, flowing into lake beds, complete with islands and shoals. It is evidence of a process much like the one that shaped Earth's surface – but the chemistry is dramatically different.

Water on the satellite remains permanently frozen because of frigid −275°F (−170°C) temperatures, and the "rocks" that litter the landscape are in fact frozen water ice. But methane (the odorless, colorless gas that is the main component of natural gas) can exist as either liquid or gas due to the extreme cold and intense atmospheric pressure. It is methane vapor that rises from the moon's chilly surface to warm, liquefy and fall as rain.

Although methane in Titan's atmosphere is destroyed by sunlight, producing hydrocarbons responsible for the moon's thick layer of smog, a surface source appears to continually replenish it. Along with nitrogen and ethane, Huygens detected traces of argon 40, which is evidence of volcanic activity. What the volcanoes of Titan have spewed, however, is not lava but water ice and ammonia.

TITAN'S ATMOSPHERIC SHROUD (TOP)

COMPOSITE OF 4 ULTRAVIOLET AND INFRARED IMAGES (COLOR ADDED)

CASSINI ORBITER

746 MILES (1,200KM) FROM CASSINI

26 OCTOBER 2004

780,000 MILES (1.3 MILLION KM) FROM TITAN TO SATURN

RIDGES, DRAINAGE CHANNELS, MAJOR RIVER SYSTEM AND LAKE BED (CENTER)

NEAR-INFRARED MOSAIC

HUYGENS PROBE

10 MILES (16KM) FROM HUYGENS

14 JANUARY 2005

750 MILLION MILES (1.2 BILLION KM) FROM EARTH

ROCKS OF FROZEN WATER REST ON A MIX OF HYDROCARBON AND WATER-ICE SEDIMENTS (BOTTOM)

NEAR-INFRARED IMAGE (APPROXIMATE TRUE COLOR)

HUYGENS PROBE

THE TWO ROCKLIKE OBJECTS JUST BELOW CENTER ARE 33 INCHES (85CM) FROM THE HUYGENS PROBE

14 JANUARY 2005

ULTRA DEEP FIELD

HOW OLD ARE THE GALAXIES in our universe? Astronomers used the powerful Hubble Space Telescope to penetrate deep into space, tracking light back through time to the origins of the universe, when galaxies were first beginning to form. This image is like a long-delayed postcard that reveals galaxies dating back 400 to 800 million years after the Big Bang.

Hubble's probe cut across billions of light-years to reveal a narrow cross section of galactic formations in the constellation Fornax. This particular field of view is relatively unobstructed by foreground objects, permitting a peephole deep into the universe. The Hubble Ultra Deep Field, left, is the longest-range telescope image ever taken using visible light. It's as if you were able to walk through a corridor and travel back in time.

This unprecedented galaxy group shot stands in marked contrast to ground-based telescopic images, in which many of the distant galaxies are too faint to be viewed. The Ultra Deep Field is densely packed with an estimated 10,000 galaxies, displaying an extraordinary variety of size, shape and brightness. Completing the image required repeated snapshots of the same piece of sky by Hubble's Advanced Camera for Surveys over a four-month period, with a cumulative exposure time of almost 16 days.

The diverse galaxies include both the familiar spiral and elliptical shapes we have long associated with the idea of a galaxy, as well as many unexpected and oddly shaped ones. Some resemble toothpicks, others the linked chains of a bracelet, still others appear like isolated gems. A few seem to be interacting with each other. The differences in structure represent the spectrum of earliest to most recent, with the earliest reflecting the chaos of the infant universe that formed them.

U

THE HUBBLE ULTRA DEEP FIELD IN THE CONSTELLATION FORNAX

VISIBLE-LIGHT AND NEAR-INFRARED IMAGE

HUBBLE SPACE TELESCOPE (EARTH-ORBITING)

24 SEPTEMBER 2003– 16 JANUARY 2004

THE VIEW DOWN A 13-BILLION- LIGHT-YEAR CORRIDOR

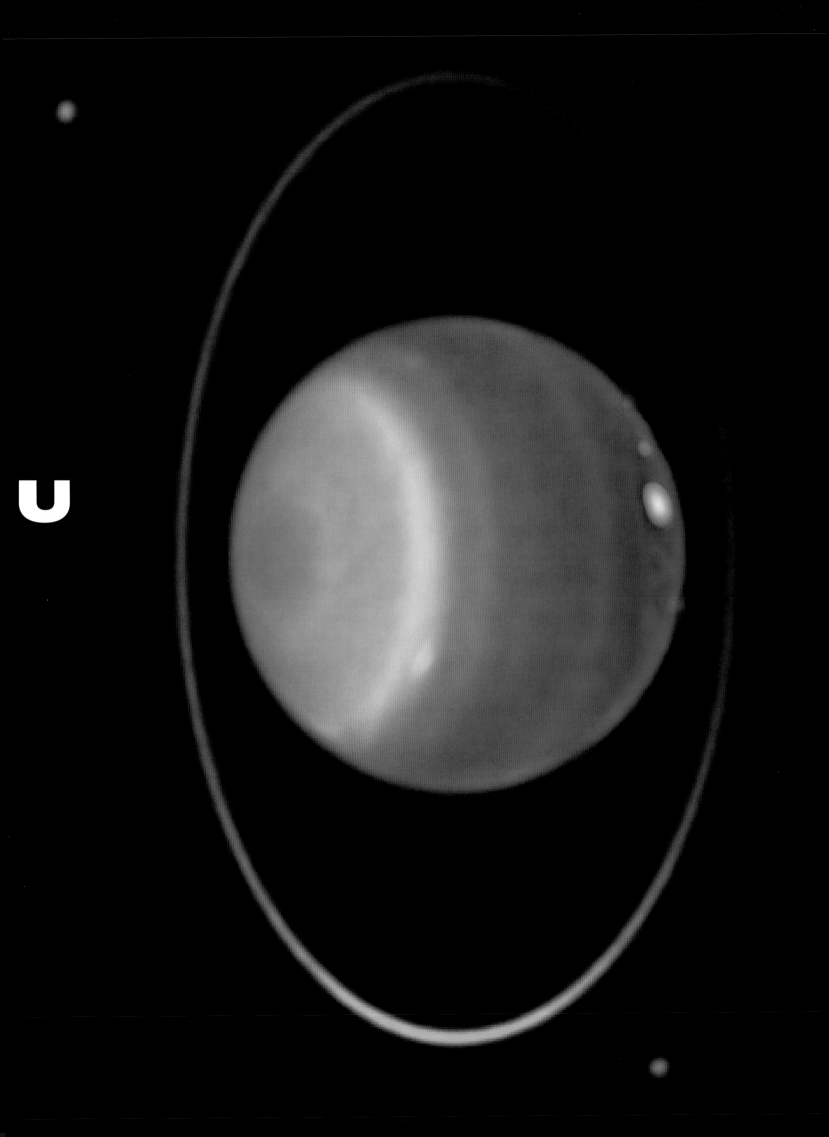

URANUS

"On the Voyager project, we used to call Uranus a featureless blue tennis ball," says planetary scientist Dr Ellis D. Miner. "In fact, it is anything but."

Uranus, the third largest planet in the solar system and seventh from the Sun, was identified as a comet by British astronomer William Herschel in 1781. Others (including his son) were the first to recognize that it was a new planet. The rings, however, were not discovered for another two centuries.

Named for the Greek god of the heavens, Uranus has 11 rings, some of the brightest clouds at the far edge of the solar system and 27 known moons. Most moons were named for Shakespearean characters, including Portia, Cordelia, Oberon and Puck. Miranda (the heroine of The Tempest) features steep cliffs and winding valleys that scientists think may be evidence of the partial melting of the moon's interior.

Uranus is a gas giant with no solid surface. Eighty percent of its mass consists of a liquid core made up mainly of icy materials (water, methane and ammonia). Hydrogen, helium

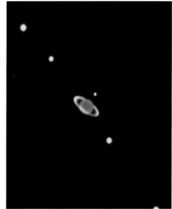

and a small quantity of methane make up its atmosphere. Methane gas above the cloud layers of its upper atmosphere gives the planet a distinctive blue-green color.

In 2004, observations conducted at the W.M. Keck Observatory in Hawaii identified at least 31 cloud features that changed quite dramatically between viewings. These cloud features are massive storms that could encompass a nation the size of the United States. The clouds, at varying altitudes, are probably made of methane crystals that condense as gas bubbles during their rise from deep in the atmosphere.

Perhaps most interesting is the unique polar orientation of this planet. Uranus orbits the Sun with its axis nearly horizontal to the ecliptic plane, like a top spinning on its side. A collision with a planet-size body early in its life probably explains its tipped rotation, which results in the two poles of this very cold planet receiving the greatest exposure to the Sun in the course of a long orbit of 84 years.

U

URANUS WITH RINGS
(LEFT)
NEAR-INFRARED IMAGE
(ENHANCED COLOR)
HUBBLE SPACE TELESCOPE
(EARTH-ORBITING)
8 AUGUST 1998
1.8 BILLION MILES
(2.8 BILLION KM)
FROM EARTH

URANUS AND SATELLITES
(TOP)
NEAR-INFRARED IMAGE
EUROPEAN SOUTHERN
OBSERVATORY,
8.2M VLT ANTU
TELESCOPE
19 NOVEMBER 2002
1.9 BILLION MILES
(3 BILLION KM)
FROM EARTH

VENUS

EXCEPT FOR OUR SUN AND OUR Moon, Venus is the brightest object in our sky, easily visible with the naked eye. The Romans named it after the goddess of love and beauty.

Venus is an inner rocky planet, situated between Mercury and Earth. Because Venus is close to Earth in size, mass, composition and distance from the Sun, it is considered a kind of twin to Earth. But it is a far different world from ours. Venus is hot – the hottest planet in the solar system, with a surface temperature of about 900°F (480°C). Venus is even hotter than Mercury, the planet closest to the Sun.

Venus has no oceans, rain or wind. It has a thick atmosphere of spinning clouds that trap surface heat. This cloud layer produces a greenhouse effect, making it hot enough to melt lead. The clouds also reflect sunlight, which accounts for Venus's luminosity. The planet has no satellites and no magnetic field to speak of.

Another dramatic difference from Earth is the intense pressure of the Venusian atmosphere. Its surface pressure is 90 times that of Earth, so standing on Venus would feel as if you were 3,000 feet (900m) deep in an ocean here on Earth. The dense atmosphere is composed primarily of carbon dioxide, droplets of sulfuric acid and almost no water vapor. The intense surface pressure is why probes that have landed on Venus have survived only hours before being crushed.

Venus's rotation is slow and a little strange. It rotates on its axis only once every 243 Earth days. Most unusual is the planet's retrograde or "backward" rotation. Venus spins in the opposite direction of its orbit around the Sun, which would make the Sun seem to rise in the west and set in the east. Venus orbits the Sun every 225 Earth days, but its retrograde rotation means that a day on Venus lasts 117 Earth days.

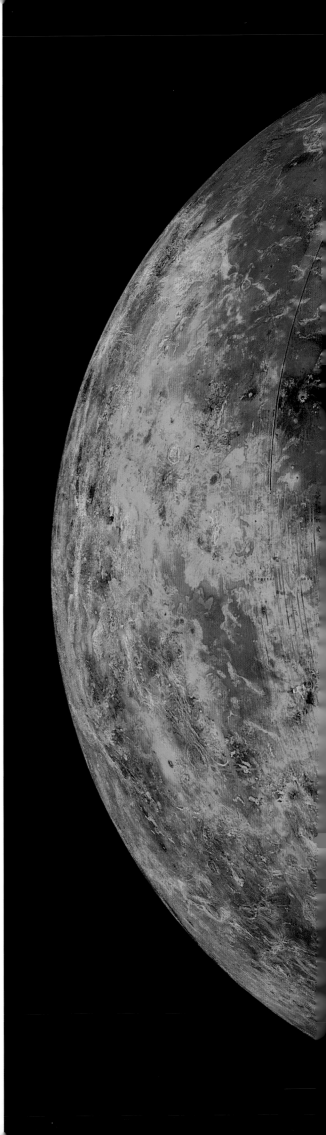

VENUS
COLOR-CODED MOSAIC OF RADAR IMAGES

MAGELLAN SPACECRAFT

182 MILES (294KM) FROM MAGELLAN

SEPTEMBER 1990– SEPTEMBER 1992

24–162 MILLION MILES (38–261 MILLION KM) FROM EARTH

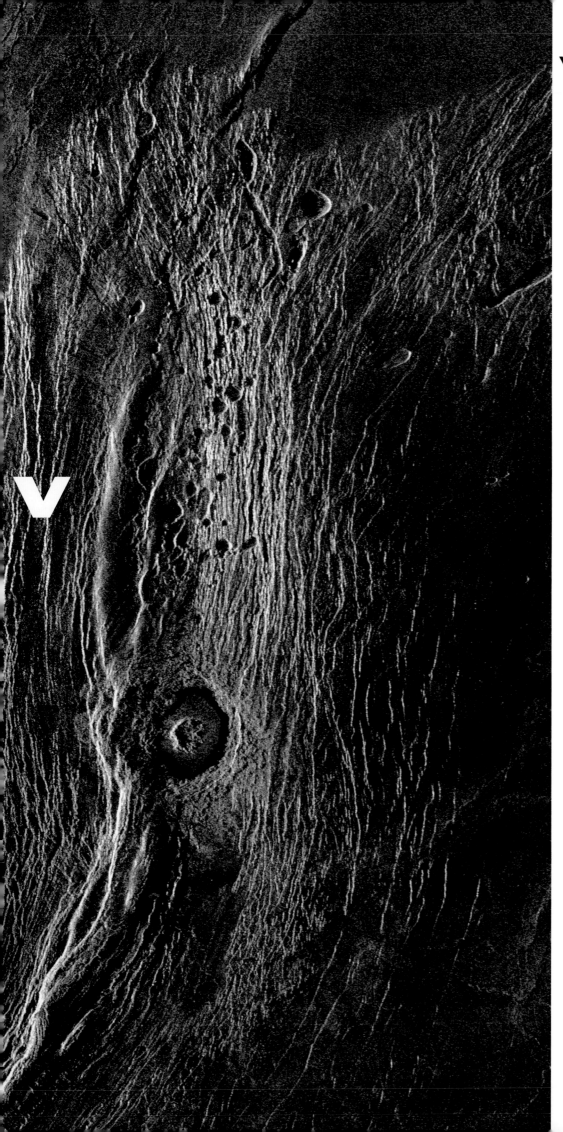

VENUS SCAPES

In detailed close-ups, the topography of Venus seems almost familiar. Like Earth, Venus has a relatively young surface. It consists mainly of rolling upland plains, with some lowlands and highlands. There are volcanoes, too, although none appear to be active today.

Altogether, there may be more than a million volcanoes or volcanic centers larger than half a mile (1km) in diameter and more than 1,000 volcanoes larger than 12 miles (20km). Much of the planet's surface is covered in lava flow. In the northern highlands, the Ishtar Terra is a lava-filled basin larger than the continental United States. And along the equator, the Aphrodite Terra highlands extend for 6,000 miles (10,000km), half the size of Africa. While there are large impact craters on Venus, there are few small ones because the dense atmosphere burns up most meteors before they reach the surface.

AKNA MONTES (MOUNTAINS) WITH THE 14-MILE-WIDE (22KM) IMPACT CRATER WANDA (LEFT)

THE 43-MILE-WIDE (69KM) IMPACT CRATER DICKINSON, IN VENUS'S ATALANTA REGION (RIGHT)

RADAR IMAGES

MAGELLAN SPACECRAFT

182 MILES (294KM) FROM MAGELLAN

1990–1992

24–162 MILLION MILES (38–261 MILLION KM) FROM EARTH

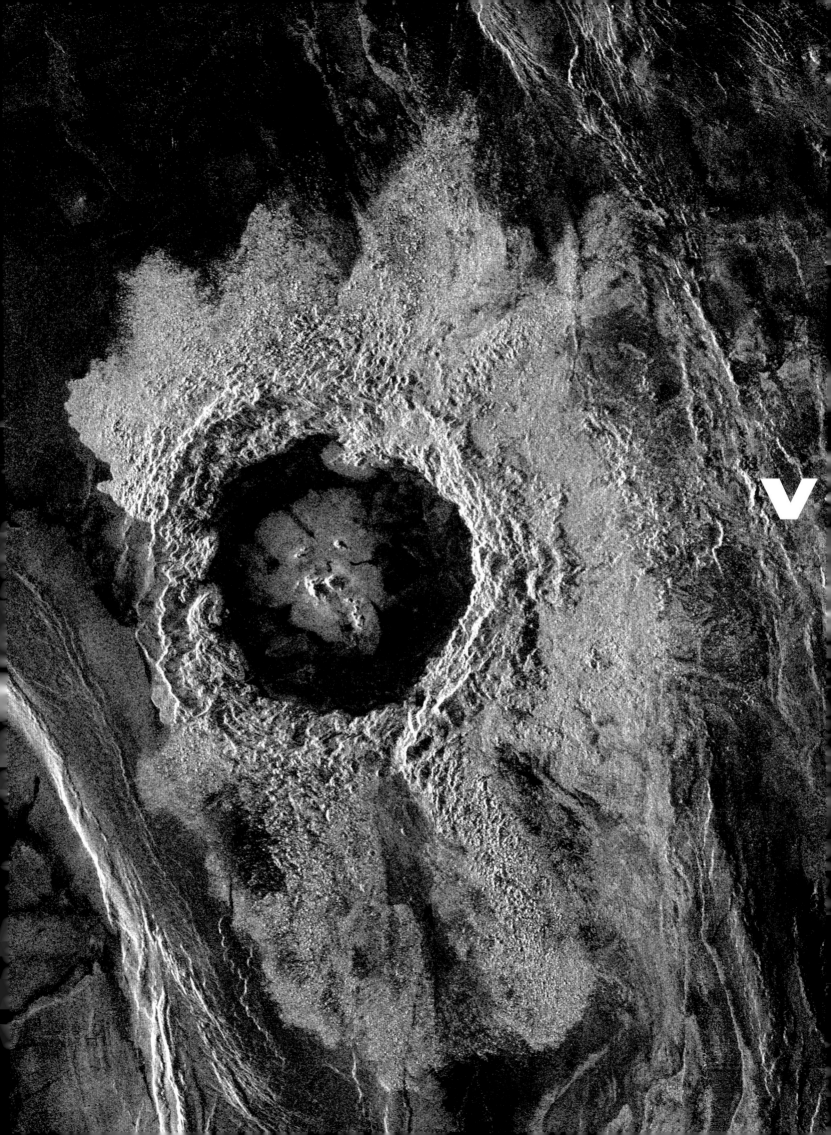

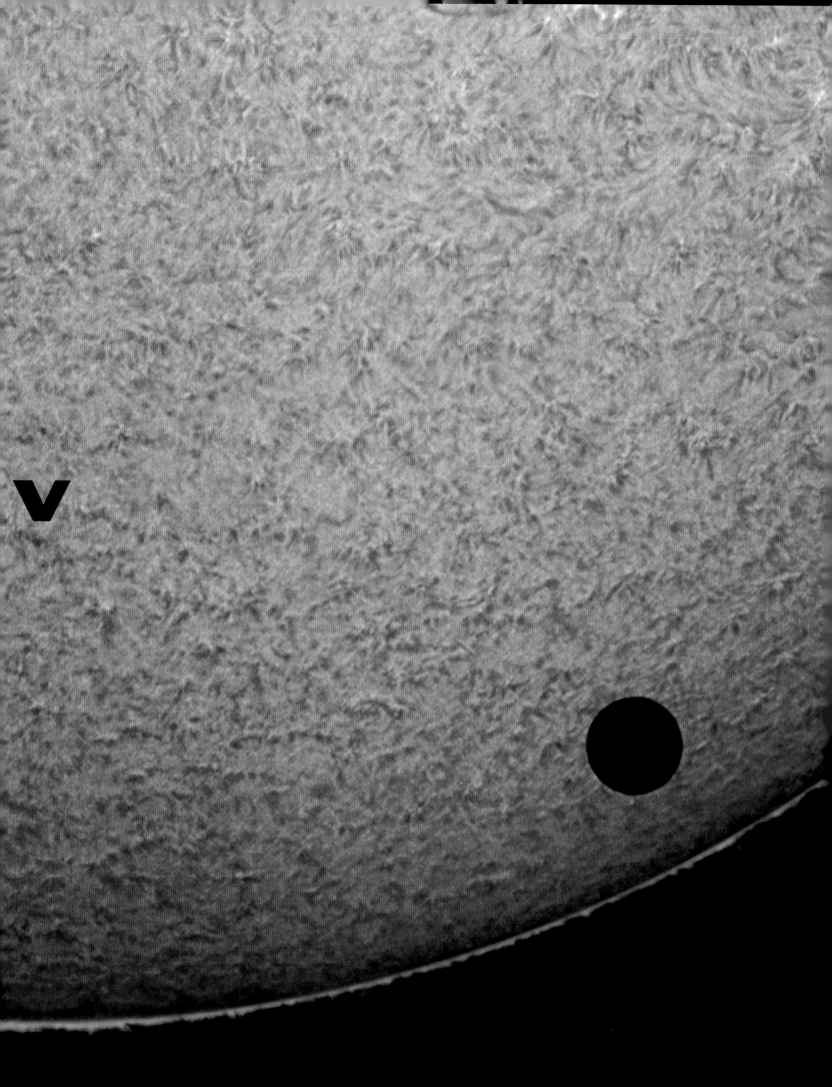

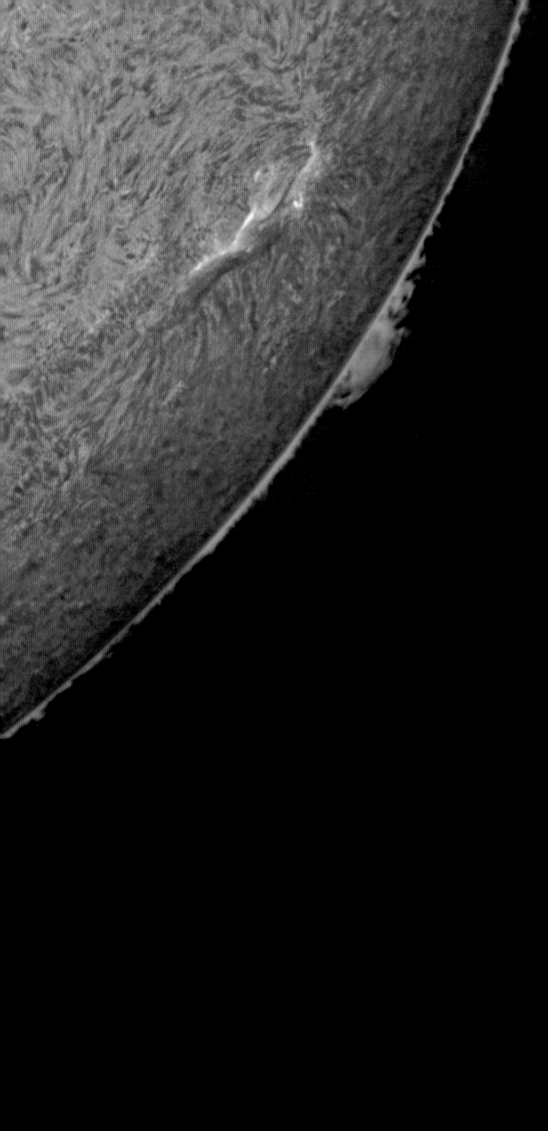

VENUS TRANSIT

IN ASTRONOMICAL TERMS, A transit is the passing of a planet across the face of a star. It is a rare occurrence, and of the two transits visible from Earth, Mercury and Venus, that of Venus is rarer. Mercury passes in front of the Sun an average of 13 times every century. Venus's transits occur in widely separated eight-year pairs, at alternating intervals of 105.5 and 121.5 years.

Since the invention of the telescope in 1610, there have been seven transits of Venus: in 1631, 1639, 1761, 1769, 1874 and 1882. The most recent transit occurred in June 2004 and took approximately six hours to complete. The event was visible from start to finish in Europe, Africa and Asia, but not from the Western Hemisphere. The next transit will take place in June 2012.

Astronomers used to be interested in Venus's transits as a means of calculating the distance between Earth and the Sun. Now transits are used to search for other planetary systems. When a planet passes across its central star, there is a momentary reduction in the star's luminosity. By studying such reductions, scientists hope to pinpoint the location and confirm the existence of still unidentified planets in unknown solar systems.

VENUS IN TRANSIT ACROSS THE SUN

VISIBLE-LIGHT IMAGE THROUGH H-ALPHA FILTER

STEFAN SEIP WITH 100MM F/8 APOCHROMATIC REFRACTING TELESCOPE

8 JUNE 2004

26.9 MILLION MILES (43.2 MILLION KM) FROM EARTH TO VENUS AT THE DATE OF TRANSIT

94.4 MILLION MILES (151.9 MILLION KM) FROM EARTH TO SUN AT THE DATE OF TRANSIT

WHITE DWARF

AMONG THE DIMMEST YET HOTTEST stars in the sky are white dwarfs. These are common stars in the last stage of life. A white dwarf packs all its mass into an object a millionth its former size. On average, a white dwarf is the size of Earth, but its mass is equal to that of our Sun.

Stars of low or medium mass, like our Sun, end as white dwarfs. First, however, they become red giants. As these red giants run out of hydrogen and start burning helium, outer layers are drawn off into space, where they will form a planetary nebula. Finally, when the helium is exhausted, the core contracts into a hot, dense white dwarf.

Over time, white dwarfs will radiate away their remaining energy, growing cooler and dimmer. It is theorized that eventually they become black dwarfs and disappear from view. However, since this would take many billions of years, the universe is not yet old enough for any black dwarfs to actually exist.

In this image of the Helix Nebula, a planetary nebula, an expanding circular rainbow of glowing gas surrounds a central, dying star. The speck of light in the middle is a white dwarf, which seems to float in a blue sea of gas.

THE WHITE DWARF IS THE TINY DOT IN THE CENTER OF THE HELIX NEBULA

VISIBLE-LIGHT COMPOSITE OF DIFFERENT COLOR FILTERS

HUBBLE SPACE TELESCOPE (EARTH-ORBITING)

3 NOVEMBER 2001, 19 NOVEMBER 2002

650 LIGHT-YEARS FROM EARTH

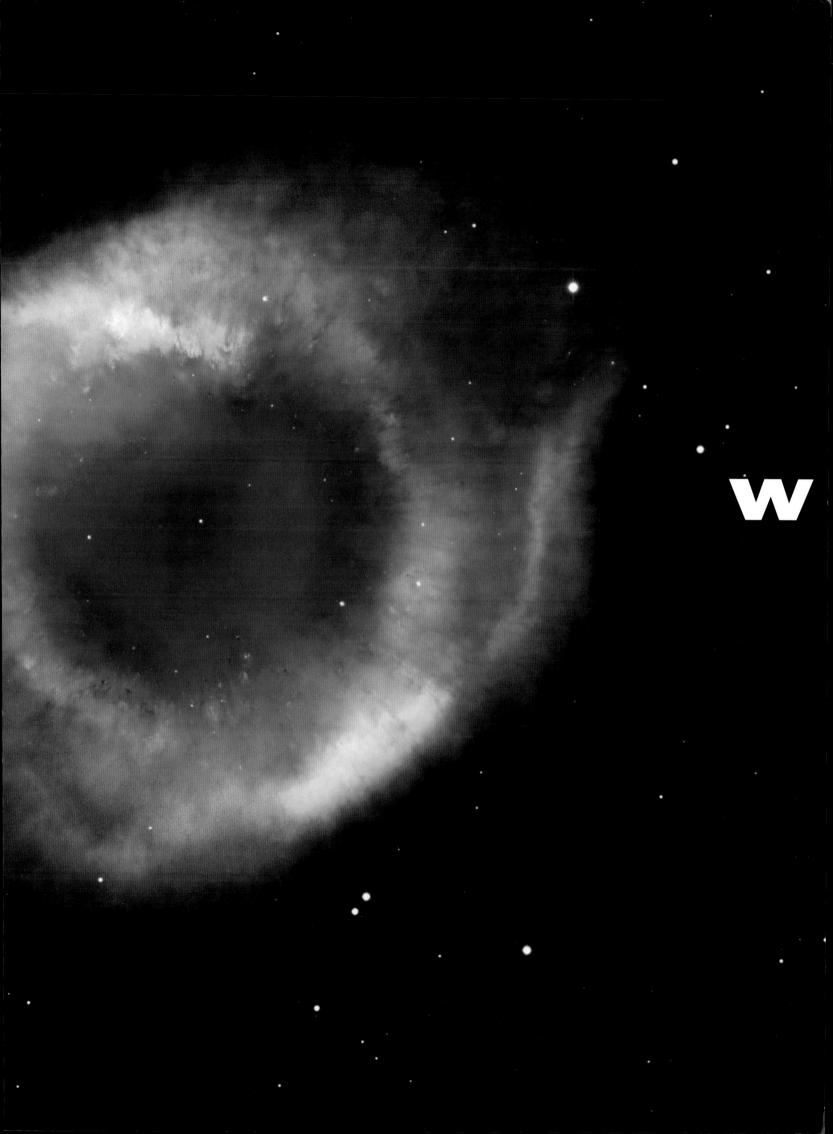

WMAP

EVER SINCE THE BIG BANG THEORY of the universe came into widespread acceptance, scientists have been trying to understand what happened next — and next and next. In 2002, in a highly sophisticated variant on one of the basic rules of space observation — that the light we perceive in the sky is light traveling toward us out of the past — NASA's Wilkinson Microwave Anisotropy Probe (WMAP) succeeded in producing the first detailed full-sky map of the universe at the dawn of time. A "baby picture" of the 13-billion-year-old universe at 379,000 years, it is both a powerful confirmation of the basic theory of Big Bang and the first record of light emerging from the impenetrable darkness that followed the universe's explosive beginnings.

Much as an infrared weather map of Earth displays the distribution of heat and cold in a clear, discernible pattern, the WMAP image captures the distribution of light emitted by the universe soon after it started to expand. Scientists date the first "igniting" of stars in the universe to roughly 400,000 years after the Big Bang. As the universe continued to cool, protons and electrons combined to form neutral hydro-

WMAP LOOKS BACK
IN TIME TO WHEN
LIGHT FIRST APPEARED –
379,000 YEARS
AFTER THE BIG BANG

MICROWAVE IMAGE

WILKINSON MICROWAVE
ANISOTROPY PROBE
(ORBIT 1 MILLION MILES/
1.6 MILLION KM FROM
EARTH OPPOSITE THE SUN)

AUGUST 2002
(FIRST FULL-SKY SURVEY
COMPLETE)

PROBE TO INFINITY

w

gen, whose interaction with cosmic microwave background photons made the WMAP image possible across billions of light-years.

Working from WMAP's radiation "blueprint" of the universe, where red signifies "warmer" spots and blue "cooler" areas,

cosmologists have been able to identify the faint precursors of galaxies, as if reading an adult's ultimate physical dimensions and contours from the cells of a week-old fetus.

Data provided by WMAP have helped scientists confirm or refine many assumptions about

the universe, beginning with its composition, now determined to be 4 percent atoms, 23 percent cold dark matter and 73 percent dark energy.

The universe's rate of expansion has been narrowed to within a 5 percent margin of error, a factor crucial to calculating its age,

which has been newly fixed at 13.7 billion years, within a 1 percent margin of error.

Finally, the data from WMAP appear to support the theory that the universe will continue to expand, giving its life expectancy an upgrade to "infinite." At least for now.

THE LIVING COLOR

The Science Behind the Images   by Ray Villard

MORE THAN ANY OTHER SCIENCE, astronomy relies on the art of seeing. The ephemeral photons of starlight are every bit as valuable to astronomers as fossils to paleontologists, or rock core samples to geologists. Because celestial objects beyond our solar system are physically unreachable, everything we know about them is encoded in starlight. Knowledge about any astronomical object is deduced from its brightness, shape, sky position and, most important of all, color.

On a clear night the stars simply look like pinpoints of white light, and the sky we see is largely devoid of color. However, a careful observer will notice that some stars have pastel shades of blue, yellow or orange. In fact, the name of the summer star Antares means "rival of Mars" because its orange hue mimics the ruddy glow of the red planet.

The universe is intrinsically much more vibrant with color than these muted shades. Our eyes simply cannot detect the rich colors spread across the canvas of the universe. There is too little energy in feeble starlight — which has traveled hundreds or thousands of light-years across space — to stimulate the red, green and blue receptors in our retina. These cone cells communicate color information to our

brain's vision center, where information is combined into a color image. The more sensitive rod cells of the retina continue to faithfully capture photons to give us a black-and-white view on a dim night.

To capture these colors, we need telescopes that greatly amplify starlight. Much more than simply aesthetics, astronomical colors yield clues to a celestial object's chemical makeup, temperature, motion through space and even distance from Earth. Planet colors are the most natural and the easiest to interpret. Planets do not glow but simply reflect light from the Sun, just like any landscape on Earth. Planet colors are due to absorption of some wavelengths of light. The cyan hues of Neptune and Uranus are due to methane in their atmospheres, which absorbs red light. Mars's ruddy hue is due to a rusty iron-oxide soil that absorbs green wavelengths. Jupiter's Easter-egg look may come from sulfur compounds in the turbulent atmosphere. This is no different from when we look at a green leaf. The chlorophyll absorbs red light. Hence the leaf looks green.

Anyone who has ever watched a fireworks display knows that extremely hot objects make light and color. Color, in fact, can be used to infer a star's temperature. Just watch as the coil in a toaster oven heats from dull cherry red to yellow-orange. Or imagine a dying ember fading from orange down to dull red. The cooler the star, the redder it is. Conversely, the hotter the star, the bluer it is. Color pictures of galaxies faithfully reveal the temperatures of these different stellar populations. The outer disk is rich in young hot blue stars. The older surviving stars in a galaxy's central bulge are more yellowish.

Interstellar clouds of glowing gas look like the neon lights on a honky-tonk strip of nightclubs. When electrified, the gas neon glows a vibrant yellow; other gases also glow at specific colors. The colors are very saturated and pure. Likewise, gases in space are excited into glowing by being trapped and heated in magnetic fields, blasted by ultraviolet radiation and shocked by collisions with blast waves from exploding stars. Some of the rich colors are from elements that are fundamental to life on Earth. Oxygen glows deep blue, nitrogen is forest green, various energized states of hydrogen can cause it to glow magenta or green, sulfur glows yellow.

The process of producing color images involves collecting energy from across the visible portion of the electromagnetic spectrum. Photographic film, video cameras and even the offset printing process all make color pictures by combining separate channels of color information. For example, film has three layers of photosensitive emulsion: red, green and blue. The balances between these primary colors can yield literally millions of hues. For purity and control of color, the motion picture industry developed the Technicolor process in the 1930s. Three separate rolls of black-and-white film were exposed simultaneously through red, blue and green filters. The black-and-white strips were then projected through the same color filters and printed simultaneously onto a single piece of color film.

Likewise, spacecraft cameras take images through different colored filters. The overlap between some of these filters allows for a truly full-color spectrum image to be assembled. But scientists also need a wide assortment of narrow-band filters that are precisely tuned to certain frequencies of light. For example, the rarefied hot hydrogen in active regions on

THE ELECTROMAGNETIC SPECTRUM Photographing the cosmos in different wavelengths of light allows us to explore otherwise "invisible" objects.

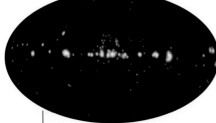

Milky Way in Gamma Rays

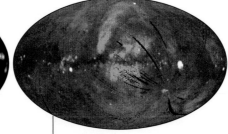

Milky Way in X-Rays

Milky Way in Ultraviolet

Milky Way in Visible Light

UNIVERSE

the Sun glows at a wavelength of 6562 angstroms (an angstrom is one 10-billionth of a meter). Like a radio station channel, a filter can be "fine-tuned" to block out extraneous color wavelengths and show detailed structure.

Some of the cameras that have returned the most spectacular pictures — Hubble's Advanced Camera for Surveys, the Mars rover cameras, the Cassini orbiter camera at Saturn — all have literally dozens of color filters for scientific analysis. These filters are used for precisely dissecting the colors of the universe from either glowing gases or reflected light.

The challenge for the science image processor is to combine all this information into an image that is a reasonable representation of reality. The rules for making an effective scientific picture are no different from the rules for an aesthetic photographic image. The image requires proper tonal range, from coal black to snow white. The full range of colors along the visible spectrum should be represented. Color, even artificially added to a monochrome image, provides an extra dimension for analyzing scientific details.

When digital imaging processing began to be used by astronomers in the 1970s, they applied artificial colors to the images. Gray tones could be assigned various hues. This made for some

garish but scientifically meaningful space pictures through the 1980s. Now cameras have become more sophisticated, and microcomputers have allowed for more complex digital image processing, where color can be controlled even more precisely.

Still, the act of assembling an image sent back to Earth from a spacecraft or gleaned from a telescope will always require an element of subjectivity and interpretation by the science image processor. The first close-up images sent back to Earth by the Pioneer 10 spacecraft in the early 1970s were tweaked in a seat-of-the-pants style by a specialist who reasoned that Jupiter's ammonia ice crystal clouds should look white, just as they do in ground-based telescopes. When the first Viking lander touched down on Mars in 1976, imaging specialists adjusted the sky to be blue because they expected the sky to be deep blue, like our thin atmosphere as seen from an airplane at 20,000 feet (6,000m). Further calibration revealed, embarrassingly, that the Martian sky was a pinkish salmon color!

Another daunting challenge is that the universe is also vibrant in what can only be called "invisi-

ble colors," those energies along the electromagnetic spectrum that are beyond the visible wavelengths we call light. Infrared light comes from warm dust, radio waves come from interstellar gases, X-ray energies come from seething plasma heated to millions of degrees as it spirals into a black hole or gets sizzled by other violent phenomena. The only difference among these energies is the wavelengths of the radiation, just as the range of octaves on a piano all come from the same physical instrument.

Light is analogous to sound, which is also transmitted by waves. Our ears can hear from long-wavelength bass tones all the way up to ear-piecing short frequencies. However, our eyes see just a small midrange of electromagnetic wavelengths, which we call visible light. Without the power of telescopes, trying to comprehend the vibrancy of the electromagnetic universe is as impossible as trying to appreciate the richness of an orchestra through a small pocket radio speaker that can't reproduce bass or treble.

Obviously, wavelengths such as X-ray, radio and infrared do not have any colors detectable by the human eye. The image processor must pull these data into the world of visual perception by arbitrarily assigning colors to "invisible" light. For example, if pictures are taken at different infrared

wavelengths, red, green and blue can be assigned to relatively long, medium and short wavelengths of light. This can produce gorgeous pictures that attempt to map color values onto invisible radiation. The artificial color can be obvious when all the stars look pink or blue. Likewise, X-ray intensities can be mapped onto colors to produce even more garish but scientifically meaningful images.

As remarkable as the human brain is, and as perfectly as the eye performs, our vision of the infinitely vast universe is greatly restricted. Telescopes, combined with computers and the talents of image-processing specialists, vastly expand our perception of the richness of the universe. Today's astronomical images are the most exquisite views of the universe humans have ever assembled. These images not only talk to us on a scientific, intellectual level, but also evoke emotions about the vibrancy and evocative beauty of deep space. Many of the celestial objects in this book appear as they did long ago and far away, so our only intimacy with them will always come exclusively through the sheer power of the color image.

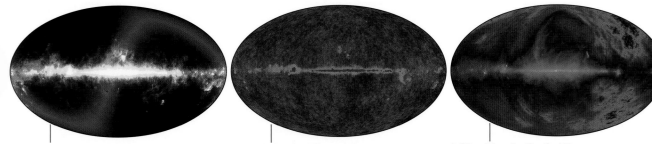

Milky Way in Infrared   Milky Way in Microwaves   Milky Way in Radio Waves

THE IMAGE MAKERS
The Mechanical and Human Heroes of Space Exploration

Lunar Orbiter 4

EARTH-BASED

ANGLO-AUSTRALIAN OBSERVATORY

The 3.9m Anglo-Australian Telescope (AAT), located in New South Wales, Australia, went into operation in 1974. Until then, most of the world's largest telescopes were built in the Northern Hemisphere. The AAT was designed to explore some of the most exciting regions of the southern sky. The telescope's imaging camera once used special black-and-white photographic plates, now replaced by electronic detectors. Color images are created by combining three separate black-and-white exposures that record images in blue, green and red light.

CANADA-FRANCE-HAWAII TELESCOPE

Operational in 1979, the Canada-France-Hawaii Telescope (CFHT) is a 3.6m mirror optical/infrared telescope. The observatory is on the summit of Mauna Kea on the island of Hawaii. CFHT was originally designed for use with large photographic plates, but today employs a state-of-the-art MegaPrime optical 340-megapixel MegaCam digital camera system with a field of view (one degree by one degree) equal to the size of four full Moons.

EUROPEAN SOUTHERN OBSERVATORY

The Very Large Telescope (VLT) of the European Southern Observatory (ESO) is actually a series of four interconnected 8.2m reflecting telescopes. Placed in a trapezoidal configuration, the VLT is located on the summit of Cerro Paranal in Chile's Atacama desert. Each unit is housed in a thermally controlled building with a dome that can rotate independently or synchronously with the other three telescopes.

GEMINI OBSERVATORY

The multinational Gemini Observatory consists of twin 8m telescopes that are among the largest on Earth. They are located in each hemisphere in order to provide complete sky coverage. The Gemini North Telescope is on Hawaii's Mauna Kea. The Gemini South Telescope is on Cerro Pachón in the Chilean Andes. The Gemini telescopes excel in a variety of optical and infrared capabilities and incorporate adaptive optics to take the "twinkle" out of starlight.

NOAO

Kitt Peak National Observatory (KPNO), part of the National Optical Astronomy Observatory (NOAO), supports the most diverse collection of astronomical observatories on Earth for nighttime optical and infrared astronomy and daytime study of the Sun. The WIYN Observatory (a consortium which consists of the University of Wisconsin, Indiana University, Yale University and the NOAO) now operates the 0.9m and advanced 3.5m telescopes. The Cerrro Tololo Inter-American Observatory in Chile is also part of NOAO.

NRAO

The U.S. National Radio Astronomy Observatory (NRAO) of the U.S. National Science Foundation designs, builds and operates several state-of-the-art radio telescopes. NRAO's Green Bank Telescope (GBT), a 100m radio telescope in West Virginia, is the largest movable man-made structure on Earth. The GBT is extremely sensitive to radio waves due to its huge parabolic dish, a mosaic of 2,004 movable aluminum panels mounted on actuators.

NRAO also works on cooperative experiments with other observatories around the world, such as Australia's Parkes Radio Observatory and the U.S.'s Bell Labs Horn Reflector.

The 64m Parkes Radio Observatory is the first big-dish antenna telescope in the Southern Hemisphere. It has played a vital role in studying quasars and discovered the first pulsars outside the Milky Way. During the APOLLO 11 mission in 1969, Parkes received the first TV signals from the surface of the Moon and is still active in receiving radio signals for the human and robotic missions of NASA (National Aeronautics and Space Administration) of the U.S.

The 20-foot microwave satellite "horn antenna" on New Jersey's Crawford Hill was used by Bell Laboratories in 1965 to detect the first evidence of cosmic background radiation, the afterglow of the Big Bang.

PALOMAR OBSERVATORY

Completed in 1948, the 48-inch Schmidt telescope at the Palomar Observatory in California surveys large areas of the northern sky. One of its first projects (in 1950) was to photograph the whole visible sky in both blue and red light. A companion survey was completed in the Southern Hemisphere with a companion Schmidt telescope operated by the United Kingdom. In the 1980s, thousands of 14-inch-square (36cm) glass plates were digitized to make a catalog of stars for the Hubble Space Telescope.

Canada-France-Hawaii Telescope

SWEDISH 1m SOLAR TELESCOPE

The Swedish 1m Solar Telescope (SST) is operated by the Royal Swedish Academy of Sciences' Institute for Solar Physics. The optical telescope is the largest of its kind in Europe. Located atop an extinct volcano on the Canary Islands, the SST boasts an adaptive mirror that shifts its shape 1,000 times a second to adjust to the rapidly changing distortions in the Sun's image. As a result, it can see features as small as 43 miles (70km) on the Sun's surface.

2MASS

The Two Micron All Sky Survey (2MASS), a 10-year collaboration between the University of Massachusetts, NASA and the U.S. National Science Foundation, produced an atlas of the entire sky in infrared light. Because infrared radiation streams through interstellar clouds, the 2MASS survey has revealed stars in the farthest reaches of our galaxy and in parts of the universe that were previously obscured. The survey has catalogued half a billion celestial objects. The Northern Hemisphere telescope is in Arizona, the southern one at Chile's Cerro Tololo Inter-American Observatory.

NEAR-EARTH

CHANDRA X-RAY OBSERVATORY

The Chandra X-Ray Observatory is named after the late Indian-American Nobel laureate, Subrahmanyan Chandrasekhar, who was known as Chandra ("moon" or "luminous" in Sanskrit). Launched by NASA in 1999, Chandra is a sophisticated X-ray observatory, resulting in images 25 times sharper than the best previous X-ray telescope. It provides images of the high-energy universe of black holes, neutron stars and hot gases.

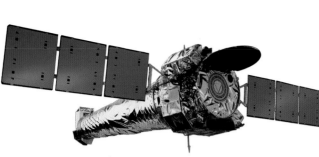

SOHO

Chandra

GALEX

NASA's Galaxy Evolution Explorer (GALEX) is an orbiting telescope that surveys galaxies and stars in ultraviolet light across 10 billion years of cosmic history. Such observations tell scientists how galaxies evolve and change. GALEX probes the causes of star formation during a period when most of the stars and the elements had their origins. Launched in April 2003, the large, circular field of view of the GALEX telescope allows astronomers to observe the whole sky and to study hundreds of thousands of galaxies.

HUBBLE SPACE TELESCOPE

Designed in the 1970s and launched in 1990, the NASA/ESA (European Space Agency) Hubble Space Telescope (HST) is currently the largest optical-UV observatory in space. At 360 miles (580km) above Earth's blurry atmosphere, Hubble sees the universe ten times sharper than most larger ground-based telescopes. Named for American astronomer Edwin Hubble, the telescope can detect objects down to one 10-billionth the sensitivity of the human eye. HST currently has four cameras that view the universe from ultraviolet to near-infrared wavelengths. Three use CCD (charge-coupled device) arrays: the Space Telescope Imaging Spectrograph (STIS), the Wide Field and Planetary Camera 2 (WFPC2) and the Advanced Camera for Surveys (ACS).

LANDSAT SATELLITES

In order to study Earth's evolving landscape, NASA launched a series of six Landsat satellites beginning in 1972. Landsat 5 and Landsat 7 are still gathering remotely sensed images of the continents and coastal regions under the management of the United States

Geological Survey (USGS). Both satellites operate in a polar orbit at an altitude of about 44 miles (705km). The Landsat thematic mapper sensors measure reflected sunlight in visible and infrared light. The various wavelengths allow for the characterization of land cover, and the USGS historical archive provides the ability to track changes in land cover and land use over time.

MSX SATELLITE

Launched in 1996, the U.S. Ballistic Missile Defense Organization's Midcourse Space Experiment (MSX) was a 5,950-pound (2,700-k) satellite in a 560-mile (900-km) near-Sun synchronous orbit. MSX was equipped with a cooled infrared sensor to detect and track missile test warheads. The sensor was also used to collect more than 200 gigabytes of data on celestial backgrounds during the 10 months that cryogen was able to keep the sensor cold. Another objective was to map the entire galactic plane in the mid-infrared. Since the coolant evaporated, sensors on board have been used to locate space debris that has been lost by ground-based radar.

POLAR SPACECRAFT

NASA's Polar spacecraft was launched in 1996 to obtain space environment data from high above Earth's poles. The satellite is in an elliptical orbit, where it swings down to the altitude at which auroras occur and then out to the Van Allen radiation belts that encircle Earth. Polar's instruments observe space particles as they follow Earth's magnetic field and subsequently fluoresce oxygen and nitrogen to create the auroras.

SHUTTLE RADAR TOPOGRAPHY MISSION

During an 11-day Space Shuttle mission in February 2000, radar measurements were collected from over 80 percent of

Earth's land mass – home to 95 percent of the world's population. A cooperative project between the U.S., Germany and Italy, the Shuttle Radar Topography Mission (SRTM) produced the first detailed, near-global model of Earth's landforms. Radar can "see" through clouds, so SRTM was equipped for mapping areas often obscured, such as the tropics. By measuring surface height, SRTM captured the dimension that is missing in most satellite images. When satellite images are now merged with SRTM elevation data, Earth's three-dimensional surface can be mapped by computer in stereoscopic and perspective views.

SOHO SPACECRAFT

The NASA/ESA Solar and Heliospheric Observatory (SOHO) is the most complex observatory ever built to study the Sun. Launched in 1995, it is located at a gravitational balancing point nearly one million miles (1.6 million km) from Earth and 92 million miles (148 million km) from the Sun. Among its 12 instruments are: the Extreme Ultraviolet Imaging Telescope (EIT); the Large Angle and Spectrometric Coronograph (LASCO), a set of three telescopes designed to block light coming from the solar disk in order to see the fainter emissions from the corona; the Michelson Doppler Imager (MDI) that studies the interior of the Sun; and the Solar Ultraviolet Measurements of Emitted Radiation (SUMER) telescope and spectrometer that observe the Sun's spectra, coronal holes and active regions.

SPITZER SPACE TELESCOPE

NASA's Spitzer Space Telescope (SST), named after American astronomer Lyman Spitzer, Jr., was launched in 2003. During its mission SST will obtain images and spectra of infrared energy radiated from dusty regions of space that are

hidden from optical telescopes. The SST has an 0.85m mirror that beams light to three instruments cryogenically cooled to near absolute zero so the telescope can observe infrared signals from space without interference from its own heat.

TERRA SATELLITE

Terra, Latin for land, is the flagship satellite in NASA's Earth observing system. Launched in 1999, Terra's goal is to access the health of the planet by providing comprehensive data about land, oceans, ice, atmosphere and life. From its orbital vantage point of 440 miles (710km), Terra observes the entire planet every one to two days and flies in near formation with Landsat 7 to provide cross-comparative data.

TRACE SATELLITE

The Transition Region and Coronal Explorer (TRACE) satellite explores the three-dimensional magnetic structures that rise above the surface of the Sun and into its upper atmosphere. The 30-cm telescope aperture collects sunlight, and the primary and secondary mirrors select ultraviolet, extreme-ultraviolet and visible light for imaging. A CCD detector captures a view of about one-twentieth of the solar disk with each observation.

WMAP

NASA's Wilkinson Microwave Anisotropy Probe (WMAP) has made the sharpest image to date of the entire universe as it appeared shortly after the Big Bang. Named in honor of David Wilkinson of Princeton University, WMAP was launched in 2001 and maintains an orbit about a million miles (1.6 million km) from Earth. The spacecraft has a pair of back-to-back telescopes that focus the microwave radiation from two spots on

Mars Express

Viking

nearly opposite parts of the sky. As the spacecraft spins, the telescopes sweep out a Spirograph pattern of the sky. Over the course of a year, this pattern fills in to make a complete map of the universe.

YOHKOH

The Yohkoh satellite, an observatory launched in 1991, was a mission of Japan's Institute of Space and Astronomical Science (ISAS), with support from U.S. and U.K. scientists. Through its two imagers and two spectrometers, Yohkoh ("sunbeam") observed solar flares in X-rays and gamma rays. Information about the temperature and density of the plasma emitting the X-rays was obtained by comparing images through filters of different wavelengths.

SPACECRAFT, PROBES AND CAMERAS

APOLLO 12 / APOLLO 17 HANDHELD 70MM HASSELBLADS

Between 1968 and 1972, APOLLO astronauts made more than 18,000 color and black-and-white still images with the Swedish-made Hasselblad EL (electric) camera, each with a Zeiss Planar 60mm or 500mm lens. Adapted for use in both the vacuum of space and APOLLO's pressurized cabins, the cameras were battery-powered, semiautomatic and, for most lunar surface exploration, attached to the astronauts' pressure suits at chest height. The cameras used detachable 70mm magazines and Kodak SO368 Ektachrome MS (ASA 64) and 3401 PlusXX (ASA 80-125) black-and-white film. To save weight on the return voyage, most of the cameras and lenses were left at the landing site.

CASSINI-HUYGENS

Cassini-Huygens is a joint NASA/ESA/ASI (Italian Space Agency) mission that will study Saturn and its moons. After a seven-year, two-billion-mile (3.2-billion-km) journey, Cassini-Huygens entered Saturn's orbit in 2004. The tour is programmed to last at least four years and will involve about 75 orbits, with flybys of many of Saturn's moons, especially Titan. The spacecraft consists of the Cassini orbiter and the Huygens probe. The probe descended via parachute onto Titan, Saturn's biggest moon, in January 2005, sending data to Cassini, which beamed them to Earth. Cassini has two cameras, a wide-angle and a narrow-angle, both fitted with nearly two dozen filters from ultraviolet to infrared.

CLEMENTINE

The Clementine mission, launched in 1994, was a joint project of the U.S. Strategic Defense Initiative Organization (SDIO) and NASA. Lunar mapping took place over approximately two months. The observations included imaging at various wavelengths to assess the surface mineralogy of the Moon. The High-Resolution Camera consisted of a telescope with an image intensifier and a CCD imager. Clementine also had two star tracker cameras that imaged background stars to help navigate the spacecraft. Its broadband capabilities were limited to imaging dim targets such as the lunar surface illuminated by earthshine.

GALILEO

NASA's Galileo, the first spacecraft to orbit one of the outer planets, was launched in 1989. The spacecraft made 34 orbits of Jupiter during its 14-year mission, making numerous flybys of the four largest moons – Europa, Ganymede,

Callisto and Io. The camera optics were built around a 1,500mm focal length narrow-angle telescope that was originally built for Voyager. The wavelength range extended from the visible to the near-infrared. At the heart of the imaging system was a CCD detector with a filter wheel for taking color pictures. Galileo was intentionally destroyed in Jupiter's atmosphere in 2003 to prevent contamination of its moon Europa.

LUNAR ORBITER 4

NASA conducted five Lunar Orbiter missions in 1966–1967. Their purpose was to map the lunar surface in preparation for the manned APOLLO landings. The orbiters photographed 99 percent of the Moon and could see objects as small as a card table. The first three missions imaged 20 potential landing sites. Lunar Orbiter 4 photographed the entire near side and 95 percent of the farside. The orbiter's dual-lens camera system recorded about 550 high- and medium-resolution frames on 70mm black-and-white film. The film was chemically processed in an onboard mini-photo lab. An optical scanner read areas of light and dark on the film emulsion and radioed the data to Earth as a continuous analog video signal, where it was exposed onto strips of photographic paper and assembled into a lunar portrait.

MAGELLAN

NASA's Magellan, named after the 16th-century Portuguese explorer who first circumnavigated the Earth, was launched in 1989. It was the first spacecraft to do detailed imaging of the surface of Venus from orbit. During the first eight months, Magellan collected radar images of 98 percent of the planet's surface. Because of the dense, opaque atmosphere,

Magellan's Synthetic Aperture Radar (SAR) system used bursts of microwave energy, somewhat like a camera flash, to illuminate the planet's surface. The SAR system was also used to collect altimetry data showing the elevations of various surface features and allowing for three-dimensional images.

MARINER 10

In 1973, NASA's Mariner 10 became the first spacecraft to visit the innermost planet Mercury. It was also the first probe to use gravity assist, a means of propulsion that uses the gravity of one planet to help propel the craft to another – in this case, Venus to Mercury. Mariner had a sunshade that was deployed after launch to protect it on the Sun side. Louvers on the electronics compartments also helped control interior temperatures. The camera system consisted of two Cassegrain telescopes with eight filters. The imaging was done with a pair of vidicon tube cameras that could take narrow- and wide-angle images.

MARS EXPRESS

The European Space Agency's Mars Express entered into orbit around Mars in 2003. Mars Express is designed to map the subsurface aquifers that may have carved the gully and channel features on Mars. The High Resolution Stereo Camera (HRSC) images the planet in full color. Separate exposures can be combined to make a 3-D image, revealing details as small as a golf cart. In 2004, Mars Express confirmed the existence of water ice in the south polar cap region.

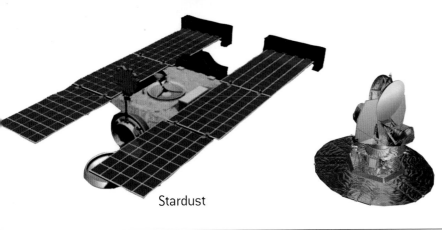

Stardust

WMAP

MARS GLOBAL SURVEYOR

NASA's Mars Global Surveyor (MGS), which entered a low-altitude polar orbit in 1997, completed its primary mission in 2001 and is now on an extended mission. To date, it has studied the entire Martian surface and atmosphere, and has returned more data about the red planet than all previous Mars missions combined. MGS's camera system collects images on a CCD array, stores them on board as digital files and then transmits them to Earth. One of its cameras has a wide-angle lens that produces a daily image of Mars. The other, a narrow-angle lens, captures images of objects as small as an automobile.

2001 MARS ODYSSEY

Since 2001, NASA's Mars Odyssey has mapped the chemical elements and minerals that make up the Martian surface. Its mission is now extended. The imaging system, THEMIS (Thermal Emission Imaging System), contains two independent multispectral systems. The optics focus light onto the infrared and visible detectors. A thermal infrared imager can resolve objects almost 1,000 feet (305m) long, and a visible imager can resolve objects the size of a house.

NEAR SHOEMAKER

NASA's Near Earth Asteroid Rendezvous (NEAR) Shoemaker spacecraft was launched in 1996 on a two-billion-mile (3.2-billion-km) journey to 433 Eros.

Mars Exploration Rover

NEAR Shoemaker rendezvoused with Eros in 2000 and imaged the asteroid from altitudes ranging from 200 miles (320km) to as low as 131 yards (120m). Its Multispectral Imaging System (MIS) mapped the asteroid's shape, landforms and colors. After one year of multiple orbits, NEAR Shoemaker was directed to make an unprecedented soft landing on the surface of Eros, where it continued to function for several weeks.

SPIRIT AND OPPORTUNITY

NASA's Mars Exploration Rovers (MERs), which landed on opposite sides of Mars in early 2004, are the first long-range robots to explore a planet's surface. These solar-powered, wheeled vehicles each have nine cameras. Three pairs of wide-angle stereo cameras on the front, rear and mast serve as navigational eyes for the probe. The fourth stereo pair is the color panoramic camera on the mast. This pair's narrow field of view and height approximate a human vantage point. A microscopic imager, located on the robotic arm of the Rover, can photograph extreme close-ups of rocks and soil.

STARDUST

Launched in 1999, NASA's Stardust is one of the few spacecraft to explore a comet. Its camera system has a Voyager wide-angle camera, a scan mirror to vary the viewing angle and a periscope to protect the mirror while the spacecraft flies through the comet coma. Stardust is the first robotic mission designed to return extraterrestrial material to Earth from beyond our moon. The probe collected dust and carbon-based samples during its closest encounter with Comet Wild 2. Using a substance called aerogel, it captured and stored these samples for its

long journey back to Earth. Stardust's Sample Return Capsule is scheduled to parachute into the Utah desert in January 2006.

VIKING

NASA's Viking project sent two separate spacecraft to Mars in 1975. Each consisted of an orbiter and a lander. After orbiting Mars and returning images used for landing-site selection, the landers detached and soft-landed at the selected site. The orbiters continued imaging the planet – Viking 1 until 1979, Viking 2 until 1982. Each orbiter's Visual Imaging Subsystem consisted of twin high-resolution television cameras mounted on a scan platform.

VOYAGER 1 AND 2

Launched in 1977, NASA's Voyager 1 and 2 were the second set of probes to explore the outer solar system, following the Pioneer missions of the early 1970s. From 1979 to 1989, the twin Voyagers yielded unprecedented images of Jupiter, Saturn, Uranus and Neptune, as well as their satellites and ring systems. The Voyagers each carried two cameras, a high-resolution narrow-angle and a lower-resolution wide-angle. The American astronomer Carl Sagan was responsible for creating the 12-inch (30-cm) gold-plated copper disc with images and sounds of Earth affixed to the outside of each probe. The Voyagers are traveling up to 90,000 miles (145,000km) per hour and are the most distant human-made objects in the universe.

INDIVIDUALS

Most images in WHAT'S OUT THERE are by large institutional ground-based and space-based telescopes. But some of the most striking are by people working with accessible and mobile equipment.

FRED ESPENAK is an astrophysicist at NASA's Goddard Space Flight Center in Greenbelt, Maryland, where he studies the atmospheres of planets. A recognized astrophotographer, he has published references on lunar and solar eclipses through 2035. Also known as "Mr. Eclipse," Espenak is the webmaster of NASA's official eclipse site. <sunearth.gsfc.nasa.gov/eclipse>

BILL AND SALLY FLETCHER typically work atop the White Mountains in California's Sierra Nevada. They make full-spectrum color imagery by shooting high-contrast and fine-grain black-and-white film in red, green and blue filtration. Their astrophotography has been published in NATIONAL GEOGRAPHIC, ASTRONOMY, SKY & TELESCOPE and Carl Sagan's PALE BLUE DOT. <scienceandart.com>

STEFAN SEIP is an information technology consultant in Stuttgart, Germany. He is also an astrophotographer who travels the world, but normally shoots from Germany's Black Forest region. Striving for authenticity, he believes that effective astrophotography is a love-match between art, physics, photography and chemical and digital processing. <astromeeting.de>

AXEL MELLINGER is a staff scientist in the Applied Condensed Matter Physics group at the University of Potsdam in Germany and a prominent astrophotographer who, over three years, took 51 photographs of the night sky from various locations around Earth. He then developed the software program that resulted in a seamless "all-sky" image of the Milky Way Galaxy in visible light. Mellinger used a Minolta SRT-101 and XD-5 camera with a 28mm lens riding piggyback on a Super Polaris DX mount. <home.arcor-online.de/axel.mellinger/>

GLOSSARY

asteroid
A rocky object smaller than a planet revolving around the Sun. Most asteroids are located between the orbits of Mars and Jupiter in an area known as the Asteroid Belt. They are primitive debris from the early solar system.

atmosphere
The layer of gases enveloping the surface or apparent surface of a star, planet or satellite.

aurora
Glowing gases seen above a planet's magnetic poles when charged particles in the solar wind collide with atoms in a planet's upper atmosphere. On Earth, they are known as aurora borealis or northern lights and aurora australis or southern lights. On Earth, the colors are produced by electrified oxygen and nitrogen atoms.

Barnard (B)
Prefix for numbering dark nebulas in Barnard's catalog, often abbreviated with a B. For example, the Horsehead Nebula can be designated as B 33.

Big Bang
The explosive event that is theorized to be the beginning of the universe.

binary star system
Two stars that are gravitationally bound together and orbit around their common center of mass.

black hole
An object in space that has almost no volume and infinite density. Its gravity is so strong that within a certain distance from it, nothing, not even light, can escape. A black hole is formed when a star more than ten times as massive as our Sun collapses and explodes in a supernova. A supermassive black hole with the mass of a million or more stars is thought to reside at the center of most galaxies.

blue supergiant
The most massive of the large, hot, bright stars. Their extremely high temperatures make them appear blue in color.

bulge, galactic
The spherical area composed of old stars, gas and dust at the center of spiral galaxies.

charged particles
Atomic particles with a negative (more electrons) or positive (more protons) electrical charge.

chromosphere
The layer of the Sun's atmosphere above the photosphere and below the corona. Composed mostly of hydrogen, it is roughly 6,200 miles (10,000km) thick. The chromosphere is hotter than the photosphere but not as hot as the corona.

comet
A body of rock and volatile ices that moves around the Sun in an eccentric orbit. Comets are small, typically only a few miles in diameter. When a comet is close to the Sun, the heat produces a coma of gas and dust that surrounds the nucleus of the comet. Solar radiation blows the gas and dust away, forming the comet's streaming tail.

constellation
A region of the sky outlined by a group of stars that form an imaginary figure as viewed from Earth. Constellations are named after mythological gods, heroes or animals. There are 88 constellations officially recognized by astronomers with precisely defined boundaries that cover the entire sky.

corona
The outermost gaseous layer of the solar atmosphere. The corona can be seen in visible light only when the central star area is blocked, as it is during a solar eclipse. The corona emits strongly in the extreme ultraviolet and X-ray wavelengths.

coronal loop
A huge arch of plasma that loops through the corona along a magnetic field line and connects a pair of sunspots of opposite magnetic polarity on the solar surface.

coronal mass ejection (CME)
A dramatic solar event in which plasma erupts from the solar surface into the Sun's upper atmosphere and travels rapidly through space.

cosmic microwave background
Electromagnetic radiation that fills space in every direction and at almost equal intensity. It is strongest in the microwave part of the spectrum and is commonly accepted to be the remnant afterglow of the Big Bang.

crater
A circular (or nearly circular) depression with a raised rim, usually caused by the impact of a comet or meteorite on the surface of a planet, satellite or asteroid. Some craters are caused by volcanic activity.

dark matter
Matter that cannot be observed because it does not emit electromagnetic radiation. Its existence is inferred by its gravitational influence in galaxy clusters and galactic halos as well as the warping of space measured by gravitational lensing.

dark nebula
An opaque cloud of gas and dust that appears as a silhouette in interstellar space. The nebula blocks out the visible light of the stars behind it.

disk, galactic
The flat disk of a galaxy composed of young stars, gas and dust in orbit around the center.

eclipse
A phenomenon in which one body passes in front of another so that the light from the background body is partially or totally obscured. In a solar eclipse, the Moon's shadow blocks the Sun's light from small portions of Earth's surface. In a lunar eclipse, the Moon passes through the shadow of Earth. Solar eclipses always occur near the time of the new Moon, lunar eclipses near the time of the full Moon.

electromagnetic radiation
A form of energy that travels through space as waves of electric and magnetic fields. Commonly called radiation or light, it spans the range from short wavelength gamma rays to long wavelength radio waves. The radiation our eyes can detect is known as visible light.

electromagnetic spectrum
The entire range of wavelengths for electromagnetic radiation, consisting of gamma rays, X-rays, ultraviolet, visible light, infrared, microwave and radio waves (in order from short to long wavelengths).

electron
An elementary particle with a negative charge and low mass. Electrons are bound to the nucleus of an atom by electromagnetic forces. An energized electron that breaks free of its atomic bond is known as a free electron.

elephant trunk
Along the walls of some nebulas long columns are created when hot ultraviolet light from nearby stars boils away the nebular gas. Within the nebula, dense globules of gas and dust resist the photoevaporation and shield the matter behind them. The globule and the protected material form a shape that resembles an elephant trunk.

emission nebula
A glowing cloud of interstellar gas laced with dust that emits light by being energized by the ultraviolet light of nearby stars.

event horizon
The outer boundary of a black hole. If matter travels across the border, the speed needed to escape the gravitational pull of the black hole would be greater than the speed of light.

flare
A sudden and violent explosion of solar energy, often observed near a sunspot and associated with coronal mass ejections.

galactic plane
The flattened area that defines the pancake-shaped disk of a galaxy. The plane contains the majority of the galaxy's stellar mass. Locations of celestial objects can be described as being above, below or in the plane.

Galilean satellites
Jupiter's four largest moons, discovered by Galileo through his telescope in 1610 – Io, Europa, Callisto and Ganymede.

globule
A dark, cold cloud of hydrogen that is often the predecessor of a star.

gravitational lens
A massive celestial object, such as a large galaxy or cluster of galaxies, that bends the light from objects behind it, magnifying the objects or causing multiple images of the same object.

gravity
The force of attraction between all matter in the universe. According to Isaac Newton's theory, gravitational attraction is stronger as the mass of two objects increases and as the distance between two objects decreases. Albert Einstein described gravity as the effect of space being warped by massive bodies.

greenhouse effect
Light entering a planet's atmosphere heats the surface and is converted into infrared radiation. The atmosphere of a planet contains certain gases, such as carbon dioxide, that do not allow this radiation to escape back into space, thus heating the planet's surface.

halo, galactic
The spherical region that envelops a spiral galaxy above and below the galactic disk. The halo contains globular clusters, dim stars, dark matter and a small amount of gas.

Hawking radiation
Radiation produced when virtual pairs of positive and negative charged particles are generated from the vacuum at the event horizon of a black hole. One particle escapes before being annihilated by its oppositely charged companion. This causes mass to leak away from the black hole, if it has no source for additional mass, until it eventually vanishes from existence.

Herbig-Haro (HH) object
A nebula produced by a protostar. The unusual nebula may be formed by gas jets streaming away from the star or by bombardment from the star's jets.

hydrogen-alpha (H-alpha)
Light emitted from an atomic transition in hydrogen appearing in the red portion of the visible-light spectrum. The wavelength is also emitted by plasma in the Sun's chromosphere.

IC
Prefix for numbers in the Index Catalog of non-stellar astronomical objects.

interstellar matter or medium
The gas and dust distributed between objects in a galaxy.

jets
Narrow, high-energy flow of matter from a central, gravitationally compact and energetic object. The jets typically stream in two opposite directions along the object's rotation axis.

Kuiper Belt
A region in the outer solar system inhabited by icy bodies that may be closely related to comets. It lies mostly in the ecliptic plane where the planets orbit the Sun. The belt extends from Neptune's orbit (2.8 billion miles/4.5 billion km from the Sun) to perhaps 30 times that distance. Pluto may be the largest known Kuiper Belt object.

light-year
The distance that light travels through a vacuum in one year – approximately six trillion miles (10 trillion km).

Local Group
The small cluster of galaxies in the neighborhood of the Milky Way. There are about 30 galaxies that are much smaller than the Milky Way. The spiral Andromeda Galaxy is the only other large galaxy in the Local Group.

M
A prefix for objects numbered in the Messier catalog of galaxies, star clusters and nebulas.

magnetic field
A force field around magnetized bodies, sometimes produced by electric currents flowing in loops. In the magnetic field surrounding the Sun and Earth, the north and south poles are linked by lines of magnetic force.

magnetic field lines
Imaginary lines that follow the intensity and movement of a magnetic field. Charged particles travel freely along magnetic field lines but are restricted from jumping lines by the force of the magnetic field.

nebula
Any diffuse cloud of interstellar gas and dust.

neutron star
A compact, extremely dense star formed from a stellar core that collapsed under gravity during a supernova. Composed almost entirely of neutrons, it has a radius of 3 to 12 miles (5 to 20km) and a mass of one to three times that of our Sun.

NGC
Prefix for numbers in the New General Catalog of non-stellar astronomical objects.

nuclear fusion
The process of combining two atomic nuclei to form a heavier nucleus. Energy is released in the process and fuels a star. The simplest form of fusion is the conversion of hydrogen to helium. Successive conversions build to increasingly heavier elements. This process requires the high temperatures and pressures typical of the deep interiors of stars.

nucleus, galactic
The central region of a galaxy, generally a few light-years in diameter. Most galactic nuclei host supermassive black holes.

Oort cloud
Large, spherical area surrounding our solar system where comets are thought to reside. The Oort cloud extends about 1.5 light-years from the Sun, about a third of the distance to our nearest stellar neighbor, Proxima Centauri.

ozone layer
The area in Earth's upper atmosphere with a strong concentration of ozone (molecules of oxygen with three atoms) that protects the planet from ultraviolet solar radiation.

photosphere
The visible surface of the Sun or a star.

planetary nebula
An envelope of glowing gas expelled by a star late in its life as it is transformed from a red giant to a white dwarf. Planetary nebulas come in a variety of shapes that offer forensic evidence about the star's late life behavior.

plasma
A fourth state of matter composed of superheated gases in the form of charged particles. Matter inside a star and most of the matter scattered across the universe is in the form of plasma.

prominence
A cloudlike structure in the Sun's atmosphere formed by an eruption of gas. Prominences have a lower temperature and higher density than their surroundings, causing them to be bright when viewed over the solar edge and dark against the solar disk.

proton
An elementary particle with a positive charge. The nuclei of atoms contain protons.

protostar
The first observable stage in star formation, before nuclear fusion begins.

pulsar
A rapidly spinning neutron star that emits powerful "lighthouse beacons" of electromagnetic radiation. This causes the star to appear to pulse at clocklike precision.

red giant
An old, large, cool star. A star expands to a red giant as the nuclear fusion process changes from fusing hydrogen atoms into helium atoms in the core to fusing hydrogen in a shell above the core.

reflection nebula
A cloud of gas and dust in interstellar space visible only by the light reflected from nearby stars.

retrograde
The atypical backward movement of certain planets and satellites.

shock wave
A wave caused by a sudden change in pressure. Examples are the shock waves created by a powerful explosion or the passing of a supersonic aircraft.

singularity
The center of a black hole where matter is compressed to infinite density and infinitesimal volume.

sol
A Martian day that is equivalent in Earth time to 24 hours, 39 minutes and 35 seconds.

solar cycle
The approximate 11-year period of solar activity caused by the entanglement and re-formation of the Sun's magnetic field. This cycle determines the frequency of sunspots, flares, loops and coronal mass ejections.

solar wind
Continuous flow of charged particles streaming away from the Sun into interplanetary space at millions of miles per hour.

speed of light
The speed at which electromagnetic radiation moves through empty space (about 186,000 miles/299,800km per second).

sunspot
A temporary patch on the photosphere of the Sun, which looks dark because it is cooler than its surroundings. The concentration of a strong magnetic field in the spot causes it to be cooler.

supergiant
A star with a radius between 100 and 1,000 times that of the Sun.

supernova
The explosive end of a massive star. The energetic output activates the expanding gases to radiate with a sharp increase in brilliance for weeks or months.

supernova remnant (SNR)
The glowing and expanding shell of gaseous material left over in a supernova explosion.

tectonic plates
Distinct mobile land masses that can make up the crust of a planet or satellite. Tectonic plates make up Earth's crust.

terrestrial planet
A planet composed mostly of rock. In our solar system the four inner planets – Mercury, Venus, Earth and Mars – are terrestrial.

wavelength
The distance between successive crests or troughs of a wave.

white dwarf
The hot leftover core of a star the size of our Sun. In its final evolutionary stage, the star has used up its nuclear fuel and collapsed to a very small size.

INDEX

PICTURE CREDITS

ACKNOWLEDGMENTS

This book could not have been completed without the invaluable assistance of the scientists and space professionals who generously shared their knowledge and helped us understand the nature of the universe.

George Coyne, SJ/Director, Vatican Observatory

Christopher Corbally, SJ/Vice-Director, Vatican Observatory Research Group

Tom Pelly, Graduate Assistant to Professor Stephen Hawking, Department of Applied Mathematics and Theoretical Physics, University of Cambridge

Orlando Figueroa, Deputy Associate Administrator for Programs, Science Mission Directorate, NASA

Ellis D. Miner, Ph.D., JPL Science Division/ Co-director NASA Solar System Exploration Education and Public Outreach Forum

Nicola J. Fox, Ph.D., Living with a Star/ Geospace Project Scientist, Johns Hopkins University/Applied Physics Laboratory

Jet Propulsion Laboratory/California Institute of Technology: Franklin O'Donnell, Publications, Office Manager; Carolina Martinez, Guy Webster, Alan Buis, Whitney Clavin, Jane Platt, Charli Schuler, with additional support from Phil Christensen, Noel Gorelick, Ken Edgett and Brian Cooper

European Southern Observatory: Education and Public Relations Department: Elisabeth Voelk, Secretary; Henri Boffin, Ph.D., Editor; Ed Janssen, Graphics; Hans-Hermann Heyer, Photographer/Exhibitions

Zoe Frank and **Karel Schrijver**, Ph.D., Lockheed Martin Solar & Astrophysics Lab

Steele Hill, Ph.D., SOHO Media Specialist, NASA/Goddard Space Flight Center

Charles L. Bennett, Ph.D., Principal Investigator WMAP, NASA/Goddard Space Flight Center

Felix J. Lockman, Ph.D., Scientist, National Radio Astronomy Observatory, Green Bank

Stephan D. Price, Ph.D., Division Scientist, VSB/Space Vehicles Directorate Air Force Research Laboratory

Michael Skrutskie, Ph.D., Principal Investigator, 2MASS

Jean-Charles Cuillandre, Ph.D., Astronomer, Canada-France-Hawaii Telescope Corporation

Travis A. Rector, Ph.D., University of Alaska, Anchorage

Bo Reipurth, Ph.D., Institute of Astronomy, University of Hawaii

Kathie Coil, Program Coordinator, NOAO Office of Public Affairs & Educational Outreach

Kevin Luhman, Ph.D., Astrophysicist, Harvard-Smithsonian Center for Astrophysics

Brian R. Dennis, Ph.D, Astrophysicist, Solar Physics Branch, Laboratory for Astronomy and Solar Physics, NASA/Goddard Space Flight Center

David Watkins, Ph.D., Program Manager, Laboratory-Directed Research & Development, Los Alamos National Laboratory

Prof Dr Gerhard Neukum, Institute of Geosciences, Freie Universitaet, Berlin, and his Team at FU-Berlin

Jan-Peter Muller, Ph.D., Department of Geomatic Engineering, University College London

John Murray, Ph.D., Department of Earth Sciences, The Open University, Milton Keynes

Martin G. Tomasko, Ph.D., Lunar and Planetary Laboratory, University of Arizona

Michael J. Mumma, Ph.D., Chief Scientist, Planetary Research Laboratory for Extraterrestrial Physics, and Director, The Goddard Center for Astrobiology, NASA/GSFC

Paul D. Spudis, Planetary Scientist, Johns Hopkins University/Applied Physics Laboratory

W. Butler Burton, Ph.D., Leiden University Observatory, National Radio Astronomy Observatory

Boris Häußler, Ph.D. student, GEMS, Max-Planck-Institute for Astronomy

Alan Bean, artist and the fourth human to walk on the Moon (APOLLO 12)

Mats Löfdahl, Ph.D., and **Dan Kiselman**, Ph.D., Institute for Solar Physics, The Royal Swedish Academy of Sciences

Bart De Pontieu, Ph.D., Lockheed Martin Solar & Astrophysics Lab

NASA/Johnson Space Center: Eileen M. Hawley, Director/Public Affairs; David Youngman and Steve Nesbitt, Public Affairs Office; Michael Gentry and Susan D. Erskin, Media Resource Center; Mary Wilkerson, Still Imagery Repository Supervisor; Juan R. Zamora, Imaging Science; Edward B. Wilson, Television and Photographic Operations; Cayce Cox, Rodney Dowell, Warren Harold, Rob Ingram, Photographic Operations Group

National Space Science Data Center: Jay S. Friedlander, Visualization Lab; Leon Kosofsky/Lunar Orbiter; Dave Williams, Ph.D., Planetary Acquisition Scientist; Michael H. Carr, Ph.D./Viking Orbiter, NASA/Goddard Space Flight Center

D. Christopher Martin, Ph.D., Principal Investigator, Galaxy Evolution Explorer (GALEX), California Institute of Technology

Robert L. Hurt, Ph.D., Imaging Scientist, Spitzer Science Center

Peter Edmonds, Ph.D., Chandra Press Scientist, Chandra X-ray Observatory/Harvard University

Robert E. Crippen, Ph.D., Research Geologist, NASA/JPL

Denis Bogan, Ph.D., Program Scientist: Cassini/Huygens Mission to Saturn and Titan, New Horizons Mission to Pluto/Charon and the Kuiper Belt, NASA

Nadia Imbert-Vier, European Space Agency, Production Iconographique et Multimédia, Division de la Communication

Peter Michaud, Public Information and Outreach Manager, The Gemini Observatory

David Herring, Earth Sciences Directorate, Education and Public Outreach, Committee Coordinator, NASA/Goddard Space Flight Center

Loren W. Acton, Ph.D., Department of Physics, University of Montana

James Irons, Ph.D., Biospheric Sciences, NASA/Goddard Space Flight Center

Robert Simmon, Earth Sciences Directorate, Visualizer, NASA/Goddard Space Flight Center

Robin J. Barnes, Space Department, Johns Hopkins University/Applied Physics Laboratory

Rachel Somerville, Ph.D., Astronomer, Archive Scientist, Space Telescope Science Institute

Mary Ann Hager, Data Manager, Lunar and Planetary Institute

Margaret Persinger, Kennedy Space Center

Helen Worth and **Kristi Marren**, Office of Public Affairs, Johns Hopkins University/ Applied Physics Laboratory

Charles Blue, Public Information Officer, National Science Foundation

Lee Shapiro, Ph.D., Head, Education and Public Outreach, National Radio Astronomy Observatory

Lynda Seaver, Lawrence Livermore National Laboratory

Lynn Chandler, Public Affairs Officer, Earth Observing System, NASA/Goddard Space Flight Center

Leslie Bell, Media Relations, University College London Development and Corporate Communications Office

Louis De La Forêt, Media Relations Officer, The Open University, Milton Keynes

Barbara Poppe and **Daniel C. Wilkinson**, Space Environment Center, National Oceanic and Atmospheric Administration

Adrienne Wasserman, Astrogeology Team, U.S. Geological Survey

A heartfelt thanks to those near and dear to us for their patience, understanding and support.

Caroline Herter and Debbie Berne
Emerson Bruns, Esq.

FOR SOLURI & NOLLETTI:
Andre, Patrick and Gabriel Soluri
Joseph F. and Jane E. Soluri
Albert A. Nolletti
David Stefanou
Gene Lynch
Kevin Fuscus
Maria-Judite dos Santos
Lisa Freudenberger
East 87th Street Tribe
Charles Arnold, Jr.
Roger Remington
Ernst Both
Frank Able

FOR HOPKINS/BAUMANN:
Jerry and Kay Baumann
Sarah Hopkins
David and Polly Hopkins
Tom and Leslie Baumann
Turner and Carlene Hopkins
Martha Hopkins
Nick and Michael Baumann
Nick and Maddy Hopkins
Ira Mothner and Linda Fennimore
Son Do and Erica Aitken
Mary Beth Brewer
Stella Sands
Gaby and Bill Scully
Anthony Blake and Kyle Hayes
Charlie Dixon
John Stark
Steven Erickson
R. Smith Schuneman
Lois Dolphin, BVM
Sr. Jeannine Percy, OSM

EARTHSHINE

LIGHT AND THE ABSENCE OF LIGHT make up the language of the skies. As we learn better how to read the heavens, we discover more of what's out there. Starlight speaks to us from long ago as well as far away, and stretches of deep darkness, where nothing glows, sometimes reveal as much as brilliant supernovas.

Shown here are the brightest objects in our sky. The Moon, in the foreground, partially masks a rising Sun, while the planet Venus glows pink beyond them. But while the objects are familiar, the view is not, for the radiant three have been photographed not from Earth, but from the spacecraft Clementine.

Where then is Earth? The clue is that bright stretch of moonscape on the right. Since what illuminates this sector of the Moon cannot be the Sun, it must be what we call "earthshine" – sunlight that is reflected off Earth (or, more precisely, off the clouds in Earth's atmosphere). That means Earth is somewhere off to the right, just out of the picture.

We see earthshine from Earth when the Sun illuminates a crescent Moon. Beside the shining crescent, the rest of the Moon is barely visible in the dim glow of earthshine. The phenomenon has been called "the new Moon in the old Moon's arms."

Earthshine is of growing interest to astronomers. It is a tantalizing piece of celestial language they seek to find repeated elsewhere in the universe – a telltale trace of other Earth-like planets out beyond our solar system.

SUNRISE AND VENUS OVER THE MOON
EARTHSHINE ILLUMINATES THE RIGHT SIDE OF THE MOON

VISIBLE-LIGHT IMAGE (COLOR-ADDED)

CLEMENTINE SPACECRAFT

1,465 MILES (2,358KM) FROM SPACECRAFT

5 MARCH 1994

238,868 MILES (384,403KM) FROM EARTH TO MOON